SUICIDE PREVENTION IN THE SCHOOLS: GUIDELINES FOR MIDDLE AND HIGH SCHOOL SETTINGS

David Capuzzi

AMERICAN
COUNSELING
ASSOCIATION

5999 Stevenson Avenue
Alexandria, VA 22304

10 9 8 7 6 5 4 3 2 1

American Counseling Association
5999 Stevenson Avenue
Alexandria, VA 22304

Director of Communications
Jennifer L. Sacks

Acquisitions and Development Editor
Carolyn Baker

Production/Design Manager
Michael Comlish

Copyeditor
Jean Bernard

Cover design by Martha Woolsey

Library of Congress Cataloging-in-Publication Data

Capuzzi, Dave.
    Suicide prevention in the schools: guidelines for middle and high school settings/Dave Capuzzi
      p.   cm.
    Includes bibliographical references.
    ISBN 1-55620-127-3
    1. High school students—United States—Suicidal behavior. 2. Junior high school students—United States—Suicidal behavior. 3. Suicide—United States—Prevention. 4. Educational counseling—United States. I. Title.
HV6546.C38   1994
371.7'13—dc20
                                        93-33197
                                           CIP

TABLE OF CONTENTS

PREFACE

Suicide Prevention in the Schools was written to provide guidelines for faculty and staff in middle and high school settings who have been trained in appropriate use of the materials. These guidelines were formulated on the following assumptions: that persons working with young people (a) need information that helps them identify the individuals most at risk for suicide; (b) need to understand the myths and causal factors connected with adolescent suicide; (c) need to be able to recognize the "profile" that identifies individuals most at risk for suicide; and (d) need to be able to use effective techniques to assess and refer suicidal adolescents.

To address the above assumptions, these guidelines are divided into eight chapters. In Chapter 1, a description of national trends with regard to adolescent suicide is provided; this chapter also includes a discussion of causes. Chapter 2 explains the components of an individual school building or district-wide prevention programs. Chapters 3 and 4 address the content for faculty/staff in-service and preparation of core or crisis teams. The importance of making individual and group counseling options available to students affected by suicidal preoccupation is addressed in Chapter 5; this chapter also provides a possible paradigm to organize and deliver guidance and counseling in the schools. (It is never advisable to encourage students to refer themselves or their friends for assistance with a suicidal crisis until the school can provide supportive, crisis, and referral services.) Chapter 6 outlines the elements of parent education sessions; this information is followed by lesson plans for classroom presentations in Chapter 7. Chapter 8 provides information about the legal aspects of suicide prevention in the schools.

Most chapters include overhead masters; these should be copied onto overhead transparencies and used during faculty/staff in-service, crisis team training, parent education sessions, and classroom presentations. **Under no circumstances should the contents be used by individuals not trained in the use of these guidelines or by individuals who cannot answer questions about the dynamics of suicidal preoccupation.**

I hope that the material contained in this guide will be helpful to schools in addressing the second leading cause of death among the adolescent population through an emphasis on prevention and early detection of suicidal preoccupation. It is hoped that schools and school districts nationwide will spend less time coping with loss, grief, and confusion after a suicide attempt or completion and more time proactively intervening with the encouragement, understanding, and assistance needed by so many of the adolescents in our schools.

ACKNOWLEDGMENTS

The author would like to thank the many schools and school districts across the country that have requested faculty and staff training focused on suicide prevention in the schools. The material in this guide was developed by the author in response to requests from schools for information, guidelines, and assistance with prevention, crisis-management, and referral efforts.

Special thanks are also extended to Karen Hafner, a master's degree candidate in the community counseling specialization of the counselor education program at Portland State University. Karen's commitment to the process of identifying statistics and other resources used to write this guide proved invaluable. Karen's background in law was essential to the process of gathering and interpreting material related to the legal aspects of suicide prevention in the schools. Since Karen's graduate assistantship for work on this project was provided by the Center for Urban Research in Education (CURE), special recognition is given to Dr. Gary Nave, director of CURE at Portland State University.

Appreciation is also extended to all of the educators and helping professionals who participate in the training needed to use this set of materials. Their interest in taking proactive measures to intervene in one of the leading causes of death among the adolescent population in the United States is admired not only by members of the counseling and mental health profession, but also by parents and families throughout the country.

CHAPTER ONE
SUICIDE PREVENTION IN THE SCHOOLS: AN INTRODUCTION

INTRODUCTION

The adolescent at risk for suicidal preoccupation and behavior has become an increasing concern for schools and communities throughout the United States. Adolescents are increasingly at risk of committing suicide; an average of one young person commits suicide every 90 minutes, making suicide the second leading cause of death in this country (Hayes & Sloat, 1988). Schools have "the potential not only to train students to identify and help other students at risk for suicide, but to provide information that will help them understand and deal with their own feelings as well" (Silbert & Berry, 1991, p. 46).

Between 1981 and 1989, fully 7% of all those who committed suicide were children and adolescents aged five to 19. During that period, 16,585 adolescents between the ages of 15 and 19 took their own lives (10 teenagers per every 100,000 committed suicide). A total of 2,029 children between the ages of 10 and 14 killed themselves; that's just over one child in 100,000 (*Vital Statistics of the United States*, 1983 [*Parts A & B*], 1984, 1985 [*Parts A & B*], 1986 [*Parts A & B*], 1987 [*Parts A & B*], 1988 [*Parts A & B*], 1989 [*Parts A & B*]).

Factors unique to adolescents make them particularly vulnerable to suicide. According to Hetzel, Winn, and Tolstoshev (1991), "adolescents experience many losses that are closely associated with their physical, cognitive and psycho-social development...Puberty changes involve the loss of the old self and the development of a new one" (p. 323). Yet adolescence is also a time of risk taking: "the adolescent attempts to prove his transcendence over death and all its metaphors" (Hetzel et al., 1991, p. 323). This duality is a major theme for adolescents. On the one hand they feel immortal and invulnerable to death, while on the other, "coping with loss is a central issue in...adolescence" (Hetzel et al., 1991, p. 324).

COMPLETED SUICIDES

Demographics

The adolescent most at risk of completing suicide is a Caucasian male aged 15 to 19. During the 1980s, 17 out of every 100,000 Caucasian male teens took their own lives. Caucasian youths were much more likely to kill themselves (annual average of 1,644) than were African Americans (annual average of 135) or other ethnic groups (average of 180 per year). Young men were more likely to complete suicide (annual average of 1,496) than were young women (annual average of 347). Twelve percent of all deaths in this age group were the result of suicide (*Vital Statistics of the United States*, 1983 [*Parts A & B*], 1984, 1985 [*Parts A & B*], 1986 [*Parts A & B*], 1987 [*Parts A & B*], 1988 [*Parts A & B*], 1989 [*Parts A & B*]).

Children between the age of 10 and 14 have a lower risk of committing suicide (one per 100,000); still 2,029 took their own lives during the 1980s. There are also racial and sexual differences in this age group. Caucasian boys are most likely to complete suicide: two deaths per 100,000 boys. Caucasian children as a group are more likely to commit suicide (annual average of 194), than African-American children (annual average of 23) or other racial groups (annual average of 29). Boys average 170 completed suicides to 48 for girls. Five percent of all deaths at this age were suicides (*Vital Statistics of the United States*, 1983 [*Parts A & B*], 1984, 1985 [*Parts A & B*], 1986 [*Parts A & B*], 1987 [*Parts A & B*], 1988 [*Parts A & B*], 1989 [*Parts A & B*]).

Suicide rates also differ throughout the United States. The western states, including Alaska, have the highest rates of adolescent suicide. The suicide rates are lowest in the southern, north central, and northeastern regions of the country (Shaffer, Garland, Gould, Fisher, & Trautman, 1988).

Factors/Characteristics

Numerous studies have been conducted to determine what personal characteristics and contributing factors correlate with adolescents at risk of committing suicide. Although some research has been conducted through examining profiles of suicide victims, much is the result of self-reported surveys of adolescents who have attempted suicide or who have thoughts of suicide—suicide ideation.

Depression is cited as a factor in numerous studies (Eddy, Wolpert & Rosenberg, 1987; Lawrence & Ureda, 1990). According to Eddy et al. (1987), "there are at least four major types of psychiatric problems that can increase the chance a youth will commit suicide: depression, manic-depressive (or bipolar) disorders, character disorders characterized by impulsivity and aggression, and schizophrenia" (p. S57).

Drugs and alcohol frequently are considered risk factors for suicide. For adolescents, there is a "high percentage of suicides (20%) and attempted suicides (15–35%) among those who chronically and excessively use drugs, be they psychopharmaceutical agents, opiates, or others" (Mulder, Methorst & Diekstra, 1989, p. 37). Attempts by adolescents to self-medicate for depression or other mental illness may account for some of this drug use (Josef, Kinkel & Bailey, 1985; Wodarski & Harris, 1987).

Family characteristics that may increase the risk of adolescents suicide include: (1) four or more siblings; (2) family discord and anger; (3) instability and inadequate parenting skills; (4) divorce or separation of parents; (5) recent family crisis; (6) family member with drug or alcohol problem; and (7) previous suicide by a family member (Josef et al., 1985: Meneese & Yutrzenka, 1990; Nelson, Farberow & Litman, 1988; Peach & Reddick, 1991).

Chronic difficulties with school and with maintaining schoolwork correlate with increased risk of suicide (Berkovitz, 1987). In addition, according to Nelson et al. (1988), "suicide attempts among adolescents result primarily from the escalation and exacerbation of long-standing problems of isolation from meaningful social relationships" (p. 32).

Method

For children and adolescents age 10 to 19, firearms account for 60% of all completed suicides. Between 1981 and 1988, 9,901 teens took their own lives with some form of firearm. The second method of choice for this age group is hanging, strangulation, or suffocation; 3,459 lives were lost this way (*Vital Statistics of the United States*, 1983 [*Parts A & B*], 1984, 1985 [*Parts A & B*], 1986 [*Parts A & B*], 1987 [*Parts A & B*], 1988 [*Parts A & B*], 1989 [*Parts A & B*]).

The third most prevalent method for completed suicides varies by age. Adolescents age 15 to 19 inhale gas or vapors third, while the 10-to-14 group ingests drugs. A small number of children and adolescents also complete suicide successfully by ingesting a solid or liquid substance, and other unspecified means (*Vital Statistics of the United States*, 1983 [*Parts A & B*], 1984, 1985 [*Parts A & B*], 1986 [*Parts A & B*], 1987 [*Parts A & B*], 1988 [*Parts A & B*], 1989 [*Parts A & B*]).

Accidents

The leading cause of death for adolescents and teens is accidents; from 1981 to 1988, 90,474 teens age 10 to 19 died in accidents (*Vital Statistics of the United States*, 1983 [*Parts A & B*], 1984, 1985 [*Parts A & B*], 1986 [*Parts A & B*], 1987 [*Parts A & B*], 1988 [*Parts A & B*], 1989 [*Parts A & B*]). However, "the Suicide Prevention Center of Los Angeles estimates that 50% of the deaths reported as accidents are, in fact, suicides" (Stefanowski-Harding, 1990, p. 329). Many suicide researchers concur (Garland & Zigler, 1993; Rosenberg et al., 1988).

In a dissenting study, Males (1991) assessed US death statistics from 1953 to 1987 for adolescents age 15–19 and contends that suicide reporting rates are currently accurate. Males found that although underreporting of suicides by labeling them accidents was probably prevalent prior to 1970s, current reports of suicides are fairly accurate.

Attempts

Unfortunately, the United States does not keep statistics for attempted suicides, so much of the data is based on self-reports. However, using the lowest figure of 50 attempts per completed suicide, the number of attempts during the 1980s can be estimated at 930,700 for children and adolescents age 10 to 19. Although the rate varies, 10% to 14% of high school students report that they have made at least one suicide attempt (Mehan, Lamb, Saltzman, & O'Carroll, 1992; Ross, 1980; Sandoval, Davis, & Wilson 1987).

While completed suicide victims are much more likely to be males, studies have consistently found teenage girls much more likely to attempt suicide than their male counterparts (Mehan et al., 1992; Sandoval et al., 1987).

IMPLICATIONS FOR SCHOOLS

The schools' role in the lives of children and adolescent continues to expand. Increasingly, faculty and staff members may represent the only positive adult figure in a student's life. As a result, school personnel may be the first, or only, adults to notice that a student may be at risk for committing suicide.

School faculty and staff can learn to recognize the behavior and factors that place a student at risk. School personnel should be attentive to young women and men for indications of suicide potential, since both are at risk—young women for attempting suicide and young men for completing suicide. In addition, nonminority students appear to be at greatest risk for suicide. Statistics and studies indicate that adolescents age 14 and older are at greatest risk for attempted and completed suicide (Josef et al., 1985).

At-risk students include adolescents who are experiencing family turmoil, suffering social isolation, using alcohol or other drugs, and/or preoccupied with death or suicide. Students with chronic academic difficulties or who are sad or depressed may be at particular risk for suicide ideation, attempt, or completion. Adolescents with a family member or friend who has completed suicide; Native American adolescents; and adolescents who are gay, lesbian, or bisexual are at risk. These teens should be monitored carefully and supportively. It is hoped that the information in this book will teach your school personnel to recognize at-risk students and help them through their crisis periods.

UNDERSTANDING THE CAUSES

The Adolescent Transition

Adolescence as a stage in psychosocial development has become more complex, more stressful, and more prolonged than ever before. Choices about drug use, joining gangs, sexual experimentation, and vocational vs. academic course of study must be made at increasingly younger ages amidst escalating peer pressure and confusing options. These choices prove to be difficult even for adolescents who are mastering separation and identity formation successfully. Successful separation and identity formation can only occur when children and adolescents have been exposed to positive parenting and nurturing models. As adults become more focused on earning a living in a country in which the cost of food, clothing, housing, medical care, etc., has increased more rapidly than salaries, they may find less time available for parenting roles. In addition, adolescents become disillusioned when political and religious luminaries (e.g., Dan Quayle, John Tower, Clarence Thomas, Jim and Tammy Bakker) lose credibility because of their actions or societal prejudice. Traditional values are called into question, and the increasing emphasis on education, which may seem to adolescents to take forever with no guarantee that they will attain the quality of life enjoyed by today's adults, may make it even harder for young people to develop needed perspective. For some adolescents using and abusing alcohol and other substances, running away, dropping out of school, developing eating disorders, sexual acting out, and other at-risk behaviors may represent their method of reducing stress and may signal their increased vulnerability to a suicide attempt or completion.

Family Dysfunctions

As mentioned earlier, the transition from childhood to adolescence and young adulthood is difficult at best. A stable, functional family can provide the support and role modeling needed to make the transition easier. Many theorists and researchers (Bigrar, Gauthier, Bouchard, & Jasse, 1966; Capuzzi & Golden, 1988; Jacobziner, 1965; McAnarney, 1979; Otto, 1972; Truckman & Connon, 1962) discuss family dysfunction as characteristic of a suicidal adolescent's family. Divorce, death, unemployment, moving, etc., are frequent occurrences in American families that must be handled in a way that promotes problem-solving skills and good communication. Individuals in functional family systems usually can make the adjustments necessary to cope constructively with changes in the family. Members of dysfunctional families, however, usually experience high stress during such periods.

A number of patterns can be observed in dysfunctional families that can affect an adolescent's vulnerability to depression and suicidal preoccupation (Capuzzi, 1986).

Poor communication skills. In most families of adolescents who have attempted or completed suicide, communication between parents or between parents and children (and usually both) has not been optimal. Family members may have difficulty describing their feelings or be uneasy about sharing them even if they are able to articulate them accurately. Usually one or both parents in such a family have not been able to role model well for their children; indeed, the parents may not have experienced positive role modeling in their families. Parents may have been taught to suppress self-expression or been subjected to bursts of anger with little explanation or basis. Children and adolescents usually are not any better at communication than their parents are. They may be unable or afraid to express themselves and parents may be unaware of the trials their adolescent son or daughter is experiencing. Sharing among family members is often difficult because there is not enough time or there are too many distractions, such as TV, the newspaper, and music, even when they are all together.

Resistance to the grieving process. Loss requires a grieving and adjustment process that follows a series of phases or stages. The dissolution of a family because of death or a divorce, changes in health status or job security, or moves to a new house or a new community require major psychological adjustments and new perspectives. It is important to integrate these experiences in a way that can lead to new beginnings and changed life-styles. Quite often, suicidal adolescents come from families that have experienced losses and in which individual family members have resisted the need to grieve and denied the feelings that accompany the grieving process. Such a family can become even more dysfunctional and can increase the vulnerability of its members who already experience difficulty coping on a daily basis. Such families may not realize the importance of grieving and the universality of such a need. They may not understand the feelings they are experiencing and may try to deny or distort the experience and the events connected with the experience.

Difficulties with single parenting. The role of the single parent in American society is difficult. Escalating responsibility, lowered income, high stress, and lack of time are only a few examples of the kinds of problems a single parent may encounter. It is difficult for even the most functional adults to cope with the difficulties of raising a child (or children) without the emotional support and financial assistance of a partner. A single parent who finds it hard to cope with expectations and obligations may have little time for relaxation, fun, and positive verbal encounters. Parent/child relationships in such a situation are bound to be difficult and a troubled single parent is likely to be raising a troubled adolescent.

Confusion in a blended family. When two adults who have custody of the children from a previous marriage decide to form a new family, the family dynamics can become quite complex. For some adolescents, adjusting to a "substitute" parent for the one lost through a divorce, a new set of guidelines for behavior and discipline, additional siblings, less personal space, or a different home in a new neighborhood or community is too difficult. Parents may need to arrange for family counseling when adolescent children show signs of depression and seem to be adjusting poorly to the new family group.

Mid-life transition stressors. Adolescence, particularly early adolescence, is a time of rapid psychological and physical change. Many parents do not realize that their adolescent children are coping with changes that are as numerous and as rapid as the changes they experienced during the first year of life. They do not realize that they need to spend as much or more time with their children than before because adolescent children look more like young adults than children in need of support, structure, and guidelines. Since parents of adolescents are usually between the ages of 35 and 50, they may be focused on themselves as personalities, as spouses, as career achievers, and as breadwinners. Often such parents, particularly those whose own dysfunctions inhibit their perspective and parenting abilities, fail to understand what their adolescent children need and do not provide the time, structure, and stability so necessary for a stable family. Such parents may be too focused on their own status and too apprehensive about time "running out" to respond to the needs of their adolescent sons and daughters. Middle-aged adults usually assess their satisfactions as well as their disappointments; this process, however, cannot consume so much of their time that family members lack the nurturing and psychological bonding so necessary for the rites of passage that carry an adolescent successfully into the next stage of young adult development.

Abusive interactions. Families in which physical or sexual abuse is occurring or in which substance abuse is problematic may be at high risk for adolescent suicide. Parents who are abusive of each other, themselves, or their children are typically low in self-esteem, stressed, poor communicators and problem-solvers, and financially distressed. Children of such parents have not been taught to feel good about themselves and to problem solve well. During adolescence, escaping the pain of such a family atmosphere or the lack of self-worth they have probably developed may become the primary motivation for suicide.

Environmental Pressures

Academic achievement. Schools and families often pressure adolescent students/children to emphasize education at the expense of developing relationships, hobbies, and pastimes that provide enjoyment and balance to release stress and renew energy. Even good students can experience pressure, threats, and admonitions to achieve even higher levels of achievement. When an adolescent whose identity is too aligned with school-related pursuits develops anxiety over the need for continued performance, that child may become preoccupied with suicide as a means of escaping increasing pressures. Death may be seen as preferable to failure or not meeting expectations.

Constant mobility. Although a reasonable amount of change and mobility can be renewing and energizing, too much mobility can result in isolation, loneliness, and alienation. Mobility often is a result of career opportunities, divorce, or a desire to improve environmental circumstances. Unfortunately, too much movement can result in depression and exhaustion. Some families, such as those living in central or rapidly changing portions of a city, immigrants, and families working for large companies (McAnarney, 1979), may not be able to exercise enough control over where they live. Such demands can make it extremely difficult for families with adolescents to cope and adjust.

High school completion. Graduating from high school is an important transition or rite of passage for most adolescents. High school graduation symbolizes the end of childhood and the beginning of independence and young adulthood. Young people are expected to want to develop more autonomy and independence from their families. Options for employment, further education, military service, marriage, etc., all must be considered; choices are complex, and decisions can have long- and short-term effects. Even though many adolescents complain about school and proclaim their joy at finishing high school, most of them experience a great deal of stress about the future. Suddenly, they are thrust into a new environment without the structure of school with their peers. Adolescents already at risk for suicide may be even more vulnerable before and after graduation because they have to face new choices, adjustments, and transitions.

Availability of drugs. Most fifth and sixth graders in the United States have access to illicit drugs. Opportunities abound to experiment with alcohol, marijuana, and other drugs and often young people are pressured by their peers to participate and threatened with expulsion from the group if they refuse. Many vulnerable upper elementary and early adolescents think that drugs can enhance their feelings of well-being and autonomy. Since problem-solving ability, self-esteem, communication skills, etc., which may already be inadequate, are never enhanced through the use of drugs, suicide-prone adolescents usually increase their risk as drug experimentation and dependency increase. Because parents often do not recognize the profile of the drug-abusing adolescent or that of the suicidal adolescent, the situation may progress to the point of a crisis before any kind of intervention. Often schools do not have prevention, crisis management, or postvention programs and services to deal with suicide prevention or drug abuse. Though communities may express concern and request diagnostic, counseling, and related services, school boards often are unable to fund necessary services and voters do not support increased taxes to provide them.

The world community. Today's young people know that the safety and independence of their countries depends on that of other countries. Economic choices, military decisions, election results, environmental problems, treaties, etc., all affect the quality of life in communities around the world. The nuclear accident in Chernobyl, for example, and the resulting radioactive fallout experienced around the world lends reinforcement to the fact that no one can be safe from a nuclear detonation, no matter how far away the detonation takes place. Some adolescents cite such fears as the reasons for considering suicide.

SOME PERTINENT FACTS

15 TO 19 AGE GROUP:

- **16,585 adolescents between the ages of 15 and 19 completed suicide between 1981 and 1989.**

- **Ten of every 100,000 teens will take their own lives.**

- **12% of all deaths for teens age 15 to 19 are attributable to suicide.**

10 TO 14 AGE GROUP:

- **2,029 children between the ages of 10 and 14 completed suicide between 1981 and 1989.**

- **One of every 100,000 children will complete suicide.**

GENDER DIFFERENCES

- Young men are more likely to complete suicide:

    1,496 adolescent males age 15 to 19 kill themselves each year (annual average for the 1980s).

    170 boys age 10 to 14 kill themselves each year.

    Caucasian males age 15 to 19 are the group most at risk to complete suicide; 17 out of every 100,000 take their own lives.

- Young women are less likely to complete suicide, but more likely to attempt suicide:

    347 age 10 to 19 kill themselves each year.

    Approximately 14% report attempting suicide at least once.

GROUP DIFFERENCES

- **Caucasian adolescents are at the highest risk for completing suicide.**

  1,644 age 15 to 19 kill themselves each year (annual average for the 1980s).

  194 children age 10 to 14 kill themselves each year.

- **African-American adolescents are at the lowest risk for completing suicide.**

  135 age 15 to 19 kill themselves each year.

  23 children age 10 to 14 kill themselves each year.

- **Other groups are at low risk for completing suicide.**

  29 age 10 to 19 kill themselves each year.

RISK FACTORS

PSYCHIATRIC PROBLEMS:

- Depression.

- Manic-depressive (bipolar) disorders.

- Character disorders with impulsivity and aggression.

- Schizophrenia.

DRUG AND ALCOHOL ABUSE:

- Use of alcohol and other drugs increases adolescents' risk of suicide.

- Use of drugs may be attempt to self-medicate for depression.

OTHER RISK FACTORS:

- Social isolation.

- Chronic academic difficulties.

RISK FACTORS

FAMILY CHARACTERISTICS:

- **Four or More Siblings**

- **Family Discord and Anger**

- **Instability/Inadequate Parenting Skills**

- **Divorce/Separation**

- **Recent Family Crisis**

- **Drug/Alcohol Problem Within Family**

- **Previous Suicide by Family Member**

METHOD: DURING THE 1980's

- Firearms were the most common method for suicide completion by adolescents:

  60% of all suicides by young people age 10 to 19 are committed with firearms.

  9,901 teens killed themselves with firearms.

- Hanging, strangulation, or suffocation was the second most common method for suicide completion by adolescents:

  3,459 teens age 10 to 19 completed suicide by hanging, strangulation, or suffocation.

- Third method varied by age:

  15-to 19-year-olds inhaled gas.

  10-to 14-year-olds ingested drugs.

- Small number of adolescents ingested various other substances.

SOME PERTINENT FACTS

ACCIDENTS

- The leading cause of death for children and adolescents age 10 to 19 is accidents.

- 50% of all accidental deaths involving children and adolescents may actually be suicides.

- More than 90,000 adolescents' deaths were attributed to accidents during the 1980s.

ATTEMPTS

- 10% to 14% of all adolescents will attempt suicide.

- Adolescent females are at higher risk for attempting suicide.

- There are 50 to 150 attempted suicides for every completed suicide.

UNDERSTANDING THE CAUSES

- Adolescent transition

- Family dysfunctions:

   Poor communication skills

   Resistance to grieving

   Difficulties with single parenting

   Confusion in a blended family

   Mid-life transition stressors

   Abusive interaction

UNDERSTANDING THE CAUSES

- **Environmental pressures:**

  Academic achievement

  Constant mobility

  High school completion

  Availability of drugs

  The world community

CHAPTER TWO
SUICIDE PREVENTION: GETTING STARTED IN YOUR BUILDING OR SCHOOL DISTRICT

Schools and school districts that have initiated and maintained a successful suicide prevention program have spent considerable time and effort planning the program to make all the necessary components available to faculty, staff, students, and parents. Sometimes preliminary planning has been done by a few individuals connected with a particular building (or an entire school district). In many instances a comprehensive committee, made up of representatives of various school, district, and community interest groups, has met to help initiate a suicide-prevention effort. Which individuals you identify to participate in planning efforts will depend on what will work best in your setting and whether you are planning for a single building or an entire school district. In any event, it is essential to include the following components to initiate a plan for suicide prevention: administrative support, faculty/staff in-service, preparation of crisis teams, individual and group counseling options, parent education, and classroom presentations.

ADMINISTRATIVE SUPPORT

Based on my experience, as well as reports from schools and school districts, one of the biggest mistakes made by counselors, educators, and coordinators of counseling/student services is to initiate suicide prevention programs and services without first obtaining the commitment and support of administrators and others in supervisory positions. Too many efforts are initiated and then canceled because little or no negotiation with those in decision-making positions has taken place. Building principals, for example, must lend their support; otherwise, all efforts are destined for failure. Developing an understanding of what suicide prevention and intervention entails must start with the building principal and extend to all faculty and staff in a given building so that they will understand why quick action must take place. During a crisis, schedules must be rearranged and faculty and staff may be called upon to teach an extra class, assist with an initial assessment, etc. Everyone connected with a given building must be prepared for these possibilities.

As noted earlier, in addition to the groundwork that must be done on the building level, advance communication and planning on the district level are essential. The superintendent, assistant superintendent, curriculum director, staff development director, student services coordinator, research and program evaluation specialist, and others, must all commit their support to prevention efforts. When administrators are presented with proposed efforts and have the opportunity to ask questions, their level of commitment is likely to be greater and efforts to establish the program can be expedited. The likelihood of extending proposed programming to all schools in a given district also is increased.

FACULTY/STAFF IN-SERVICE

Since teachers and other faculty and staff usually learn of a student's suicidal preoccupation before the school counselor or another member of the core or crisis team is informed, *all* faculty and staff must be included in building and/or district level in-service on adolescent suicide. Teachers, aides, secretaries, administrators, custodians, bus drivers, food service personnel, librarians, school social workers all come in contact with adolescents at risk for suicide. It is imperative that all of these people be educated about adolescent suicide and building and district policies and programs for prevention, crisis management, and postvention. When a young person reaches out to a trusted adult, that adult must have a clear understanding and a considerable amount of self-confidence to know exactly what to say and do and what *not* to say and do.

Many schools and school districts have actually precipitated suicide attempts by not providing for faculty/staff in-service on the topic before introducing discussion among student groups. When middle and high school students participate in educational programs on the topic of adolescent suicide, many of them realize that they, and some of their friends, are at risk and they turn to adults they respect for assistance. Adults in the school who do not know what to do and who have not had the opportunity to ask questions may be unable to help a student and may fail to make appropriate comments and decisions. Highly stressed, depressed, suicidal adolescents do not have the perspective to realize that adults are uncomfortable with the idea of suicide and don't know how to respond. Adolescents may come away from the encounter feeling that the adult has been disapproving. When a trusted adult who was seen as a suicidal adolescent's last link to society responds awkwardly or not at all, the adolescent may view the encounter as "the last straw."

IT IS UNETHICAL AND DANGEROUS NOT TO PREPARE SCHOOL FACULTY AND STAFF BEFORE PRESENTATING INFORMATION ON SUICIDE TO THE STUDENTS. LACK OF PREPARATION COULD BECOME THE BASIS FOR LEGAL ACTION BY PARENTS AND FAMILY MEMBERS. The content for necessary in-service will be presented later in this discussion.

PREPARATION OF CRISIS TEAMS

Many schools have "crisis" or "core" teams composed of faculty, staff, and parents connected with a particular building. These teams often exist in conjunction with a suicide prevention and intervention effort necessary to cope with the drug problem among the young people in today's schools. Such teams usually consist of some combination of teachers, counselors, parents, social workers, school psychologists, school nurses, and school administrators. Usually these teams have been educated about the signs in adolescents at risk for substance use and know how to use appropriate communication, diagnostic, and intervention skills necessary to begin the long-term process of recovery from alcoholism and other addictions. With education beyond what is provided during faculty/staff in-service for substance abuse efforts, as well as additional supervision and evaluation of clinical skills, a "core" or "crisis" team can be taught how to facilitate a school's prevention efforts and how to respond to a student already experiencing a suicidal crisis or in need of postvention efforts. In addition, such a team can prepare a policy statement that covers prevention, crisis management, and postvention efforts. Such a policy could be adopted in other schools; in reality, except for specifics connected with a given building, the same policy statement should be adopted and followed throughout a school district. It is important to realize that everyone who is called on to assist a suicidal adolescent must know what to do. Confusion or uncertainty about the chain of command or procedures for notifying parents can result in delays and interfere with efforts to save a young person's life.

INDIVIDUAL AND GROUP COUNSELING OPTIONS

Before giving students any information about suicide and suicide-prevention efforts in a school, arrangements must be made for the individual and group counseling services that will be needed by those who seek assistance for themselves or their friends. Unless such counseling options are available, any effort at prevention, crisis management, or postvention is doomed to failure. This may present a problem to school personnel, particularly at the secondary level, unless administrators are willing to free counselors from scheduling, hall monitoring, and other duties not related to their primary role as counselor. Working with suicidal adolescents requires a long-term commitment on the part of those interested in intervening. No counselor, psychologist, or social worker can undo the experiences and self-perceptions of a lifetime without providing consistent, intensive opportunities for counseling.

If the school district or school cannot commit to providing counseling, then arrangements for referral to community agencies and private practitioners must be made. It is essential to provide adolescents and their families with a variety of referral possibilities along with information on fee schedules. Whether the school district will be liable for the cost of such counseling if the referral is made by the school should be explored by school or district legal counsel. The dilemma, of course, is that if an adolescent who has been identified as suicidal is not counseled, the likelihood is high that the student will make a suicide attempt. If the school is aware of a teenager's suicidal preoccupation and does not act in the best interests of such a teenager, families may bring suit against the district later. (Legal issues will be discussed later in this guide.)

PARENT EDUCATION

Parents of students in a school in which a suicide-prevention program is to be initiated should be involved in the school's efforts to educate, identify, and assist young people in this respect. Parents have a right to understand why the school is taking such steps and what the components of a school-wide effort will be. Evening or late afternoon parent education efforts can be constructive and can engender additional support for a school or school district. Parents need to know the same information as faculty and staff with respect to adolescent suicide. They will be more likely to turn to the school for assistance if they know about the school's interest in adolescent suicide prevention, have had an opportunity to ask questions about their adolescent sons' and daughters' behavior, and have been reassured about the quality and safety of the school's efforts.

CLASSROOM PRESENTATIONS

Debate about the safety of adolescent suicide-prevention programs that seek to educate adolescents continues. This debate is similar to the one that emerged years ago when schools initiated staff development and classroom presentations on the topic of physical and sexual abuse. A number of experts advocate education and discussion efforts that are focused on students in conjunction with a school-wide suicide-prevention effort (Capuzzi, 1986; Capuzzi & Golden, 1988; Curran, 1987; Ross, 1980; Sudak, Ford, & Rushforth, 1984). Providing adolescents with an appropriate forum in which they can receive accurate information, ask questions, and learn about how to find help for themselves and their friends does not precipitate suicidal preoccupation or attempts (Capuzzi, 1988). Since newspaper and television reports of individual and cluster suicides do not usually include adequate education on the topic, and since many films unrealistically present or romanticize the act of suicide, schools should address the problem in a way that provides information and encourages young people to reach out for help. A carefully prepared and well-presented classroom presentation made by a member of the school's core team (or another presenter who has expertise on the topic) is essential. Such a presentation should include information on causes, myths, symptoms and how to get help through the school. *Under no circumstances should adolescents be shown a suicide plan.* In addition, on the elementary level, school faculty should not present programs on suicide prevention; their efforts are better focused on developmental counseling and classroom presentations directed at helping children overcome traits (such as low self-esteem or poor communication skills) that may put them at risk for suicidal behavior later. Although these efforts should be continued through secondary education, middle and high school students are better served through presentations that address adolescent suicide directly. (Middle and high school students almost always have direct or indirect experience with suicide and appreciate the opportunity to get information and ask questions.)

SUICIDE PREVENTION: GETTING STARTED IN YOUR BUILDING OR SCHOOL DISTRICT

- **Planning efforts**

- **Administrative support**

- **Faculty/staff in-service**

- **Preparation of crisis teams**

- **Individual and group counseling options**

- **Parent education**

- **Classroom presentations**

CHAPTER THREE
SUICIDE PREVENTION: WHAT FACULTY AND STAFF NEED TO KNOW

The most effective tool in preventing suicide is knowledge. Since 90% of those adolescents who attempt suicide warn of their plans, everyone in a school must be able to recognize the signs and know what to do about them. This section is intended for use in faculty/staff in-service. This in-service should include faculty, administrators, secretaries, bus drivers, custodians, and food service personnel since youth at risk for suicide may reach out to any trusted adult connected with their particular school building. The in-service should be conducted by the building counselor and other members of the school or school district crisis team (see the subsequent section on crisis management).

It is unethical and dangerous for an adult to attempt an adolescent's suicide-prevention effort in any context unless the adult has been prepared in advance. Generally, it takes a minimum of two full days to prepare teachers and other staff to play their roles in a total school suicide-prevention program. Additional time is required to prepare core or crisis teams and to develop a written plan of action for suicide prevention, crisis management, and postvention. Some schools prefer that everyone spend two full days of staff development on the topic; others provide one day for the entire faculty and staff and the second day only for members of the core or crisis team.

The purpose of such in-service efforts is to sensitize each adult to the problem of adolescent suicide and the school's intervention role so that each adult can identify at-risk students and help refer those students to the school counselor and other members of core or crisis teams. (**Under no circumstances are faculty and staff to provide counseling or risk-assessment services; these can only be offered by someone with appropriate expertise.**) All adults in a setting in which preventive education is presented to adolescents must, at a minimum, understand the myths, the profile of the potential attempter, and the guidelines for making referrals.

The following information will provide the basis for faculty and staff in-service education (most groups find the information in the introductory section on trends and causes of great interest; begin with the information in that section if time permits). Obviously, it is not possible to address *all* suicide-related issues here and **the material should not be used by someone who has not been trained in the use of the curriculum because of the questions in-service group**

participants ask about suicidal dynamics, diagnosis, and the counseling/ therapy process. As noted earlier, the building counselor and other members of a crisis team should conduct this in-service.

UNDERSTANDING THE MYTHS

It is important to disqualify myths and misconceptions surrounding adolescent suicide at the beginning of any initiative to provide prevention, crisis management, and postvention services. Some of the most commonly cited misconceptions include the following (Capuzzi, 1988):

1. **Adolescents who talk about suicide never attempt suicide.** This is probably one of the most widely believed myths. All suicidal adolescents try (either verbally or nonverbally) to let a friend, parent, or teacher know that life seems to be too difficult to bear. Since a suicide attempt is a cry for help, always take verbal threats seriously. Never assume that such threats are made only to attract attention or manipulate others. It is better to respond and enlist the aid of a professional than to risk the loss of a life.

2. **Suicide happens with no warning.** Suicidal adolescents leave numerous hints and warnings about their intentions. Clues can be verbal or in the form of such gestures as taking a few sleeping pills, becoming accident prone, reading stories focused on death and violence, etc. Quite often, the suicidal adolescent lacks a large social support network. As stress escalates and options other than suicide seem few, suicidal adolescents may withdraw from an already small circle of friends, making it more difficult for others to notice warning signs.

3. **Adolescents from affluent families attempt or complete suicide more often than adolescents from poor families.** This is not so. Suicide is evenly divided among socioeconomic groups.

4. **Once an adolescent is suicidal, he or she is suicidal forever.** Most adolescents are suicidal for a limited period of time. In my experience, the 24- to 72-hour period around the peak of the "crisis" is the most dangerous. If counselors and other mental health professionals can monitor the adolescent during a crisis period and help place him or her into long-term counseling/therapy, there is a strong possibility that the adolescent will never have another suicidal crisis. The more effort that is made to help an adolescent identify stressors and develop problem-solving skills during this post-suicidal crisis period and the more time that passes, the better the prognosis.

5. **If an adolescent attempts suicide and survives, he or she will never make an additional attempt.** There is a difference between an adolescent who experiences a suicidal crisis but does not attempt suicide, as in the example above, and the adolescent who actually makes an attempt. An adolescent who carries through with an attempt has identified a plan, had access to the means, and maintained a high enough energy level to follow through. He or she may decide to try again. If counseling/therapy has not taken place or has not been successful during the period following an attempt, additional attempts may be made. Most likely, each follow-up attempt will become more lethal.

6. **Adolescents who attempt or complete suicide always leave notes.** Only a small percentage of suicidal adolescents leave notes. This is a common myth and one of the reasons why many deaths are deemed accidents by friends, family members, physicians, and investigating officers when suicide has actually taken place.

7. **Most adolescent suicides happen late at night or during the predawn hours.** This myth is not true for the simple reason that most suicidal adolescents actually want help. Mid to late morning and mid to late afternoon are the periods when most attempts are made since a family member or friend is more likely to be around to intervene than would be the case late at night or very early in the morning.

8. **Never use the word suicide when talking to adolescents, because using the word gives some adolescents the idea.** This is simply not true; you cannot put the idea of suicide into the mind of an adolescent who is not suicidal. If an adolescent is suicidal and you use the word, it can help that adolescent verbalize feelings of despair and assist with establishing rapport and trust. If a suicidal adolescent thinks you know he or she is suicidal and realizes you are afraid to approach the subject, it can contribute to the adolescent's feelings of despair and helplessness.

9. **Every adolescent who attempts suicide is depressed.** Depression is common in a suicidal adolescent but it is not always a component. Many adolescents simply want to escape their current circumstances and do not have the problem-solving skills to consider alternatives.

10. **Suicide is hereditary.** Suicide tends to run in families, similar to physical and sexual abuse. This fact has led to the development of the myth. But suicide is not genetically inherited. Members of families, however, do share the same emotional climate since children tend to model their behavior on that of their parents. The suicide of one family member tends to increase the risk among other family members that suicide will be viewed as an appropriate way to solve one's problems.

    In conjunction with this myth, it should be noted that endogenous depression can be inherited. Because of the connection between depression and suicide, many have mistakenly come to the belief that suicide can be genetically inherited.

RECOGNIZING THE PROFILE

A number of experts believe that about 90% of the adolescents who complete suicide (and lethal first attempts can result in completions) give cues to those around them in advance (Capuzzi & Golden, 1988; Curran, 1987; Davis, 1983; Hafen & Frandsen, 1986; Hussain & Vandiver, 1984; Johnson & Maile, 1987). The number of cues or hints will depend on the adolescent since each adolescent has a unique familial and social history. It is important for adults (and young people as well) to recognize the signs and symptoms so that they can interview. A comment such as, "I talked with her a few days ago and she was fine—I am so shocked to learn of her death" may mean that no one was aware of the warning signs. One of the essential components of any staff development effort is teaching people to recognize the suicidal or potentially suicidal adolescent so that referral and intervention can take place. Behavioral clues, verbal clues, cognitive cues, and personality traits are described below.

Behaviors

Lack of concern about personal welfare. Some suicidal adolescents may not be able to talk about their problems or give verbal hints that they are considering suicide. Sometimes such adolescents become unconcerned with their personal safety in the hope that someone will take notice. Experimenting with medication, accepting "dares" from friends, reckless driving, carving initials into the skin of forearms may all be ways of "gesturing" or letting others know, "I am in pain and don't know how to continue through life if nothing changes."

Changes in social patterns. Relatively unusual or sudden changes in an adolescent's social behavior can provide strong cues that such a young person is feeling desperate. A cooperative teenager may suddenly start breaking the "house rules" parents have never had to worry about enforcing. An involved adolescent may begin to withdraw from activities at school or may end long-term friendships with school- and community-related peers. A stable, easy-going teenager may start arguing with teachers, employers, or other significant adults with whom conflict had never been experienced. Such pattern changes should be noted and discussed with an adolescent who does not seem to be behaving as he or she has in the past.

A decline in school achievement. Many times, adolescents who are becoming more and more depressed and preoccupied with suicidal thoughts are unable to spend time on their schoolwork. If such an adolescent has generally maintained a certain grade point average, loss of interest in academic pursuits can be a strong indication that something is wrong. The key to assessing such a situation is how long the decline lasts.

Difficulty in concentrating. Suicidal adolescents usually experience marked changes in thinking and logic. As stress and discomfort escalate, logical problem solving and reasoning become more difficult. As these processes become more confused and convoluted, it becomes easier and easier to stay focused on suicide as the only solution. "It may become more and more obvious that the adolescent's attention span is shorter and that verbal comments bear little relationship to the topic of a conversation" (Capuzzi, 1988, p. 6).

Altered eating and sleeping patterns. Sudden increases or decreases in appetite and weight, difficulty with sleeping or wanting to sleep all the time can indicate an increasing preoccupation with suicidal thoughts. These altered patterns offer strong evidence that something is wrong and that assistance is required.

Attempts to put personal affairs in order or to make amends. Often, once a suicide plan and decision have been reached, adolescents will make "last-minute" efforts to put their personal affairs in order. These efforts may take a variety of directions: attempts to make amends in relation to a troubled relationship, final touches on a project, reinstatement of an old or neglected friendship, the giving away of prized possessions.

Use or abuse of alcohol or drugs. Sometimes troubled adolescents use or abuse alcohol or other drugs to lessen their feelings of despair or discontent. Initially, they may believe that the drug enhances their ability to cope and increases their feeling of self-esteem. Unfortunately, drug abuse decreases the ability to communicate accurately and problem solve rationally. Thinking patterns become more skewed, impulse control lessens, and option identification decreases. Rapid onset of involvement with illicit or over-the-counter drugs is indicative of difficulty with relationships, problem solving, and the ability to share feelings and communicate them to others.

Unusual interest in how others are feeling. Suicidal adolescents often express considerable interest in how others are feeling. Since they are in pain, but may be unable to express their feelings and ask for help, they may reach out to peers (or adults) who seem to need help.

Such responsiveness may become a full-time pastime and serve to lessen preoccupation with self and to serve as a vehicle for communicating, "I wish you would ask me about my pain" or "Can't you see that I need help too?"

Preoccupation with death and violence themes. Reading books or poetry in which death, violence, or suicide is the predominating theme can become the major interest of an adolescent who is becoming increasingly preoccupied with suicide. Such adolescents may be "undecided" about the possibility of choosing death over life and may be working through the aspects of such a decision with such reading. Other examples of such preoccupation can include listening to violent music; writing short stories focused on death, dying, and loss; drawing or sketching that emphasizes destruction; or watching movies that emphasize self-destruction or the destruction of others.

Sudden improvement after a period of depression. Suicidal adolescents often fool parents, teachers, and friends by appearing to be dramatically improved, in a very short period of time, after a period of prolonged depression. This improvement can sometimes take place overnight or during a 24-hour period and encourages friends and family who interpret such a change as a positive sign. It is not unusual for a change, such as the one described above, to be the result of an at-risk adolescent's decision to commit suicide and formulation of a concrete suicide plan. It may mean that the suicide attempt (and the potential of completion) is imminent and that the danger and crisis are peaking. Family and friends must remember that it is not really logical for a depression to disappear that quickly. It takes time, effort, and, at times, medical assistance to improve coping skills and lessen feelings of depression, just as it took time (months or years) to develop nonadaptive responses to people and circumstances and feelings of hopelessness.

Sudden or increased promiscuity. It is not unusual for an adolescent to experiment with sex during periods of suicidal preoccupation in an attempt to refocus attention or lessen feelings of isolation. Unfortunately, doing so sometimes complicates circumstances because of an unplanned pregnancy or increased feelings of guilt.

Verbal Cues

As noted by Schneidman, Farbverow, and Litman (1976) verbal statements can provide cues to self-destructive intentions. Such statements should be assessed and considered in relation to behavioral signs, changes in thinking patterns, motivations, personality traits, etc. There is no "universal" language or "style" for communicating suicidal intentions. Some adolescents will say openly and directly: "I am going to commit suicide" or "I am thinking of taking my life." Others will be far less direct and make statements such as: "I'm going home," "I wonder what death is like," "I'm tired," "She'll be sorry for how she's treated me," or "Someday I'll show everyone just how serious I am about some of the things I've said."

The important thing for counselors, parents, teachers, and friends to remember is that, when someone says something that could be interpreted in a number of ways, it is always best to ask what the person means. It is not a good idea to make assumptions about what a statement means or to minimize the importance of what is said. Suicidal adolescents often have a history of finding it hard to communicate feelings and ask for support. Indirect statements may be made in the hope that someone will respond with support and interest and provide or facilitate a referral for professional assistance.

Thinking Patterns and Motivations

In addition to the areas previously described, thinking patterns and motivations of suicidal adolescents can be assessed and evaluated. For such an assessment to occur, one needs to learn more about the adolescent and about changes in his or her cognitive set and distortions of logic and problem-solving ability. As noted by Velkoff and Huberty (1988), the motivations of suicidal adolescents can be understood more readily when suicide is viewed as fulfilling one of three primary functions: (a) an **avoidance function**, to protect the individual from the pain perceived to be associated with a relationship or set of circumstances; (b) a **control function**, which enables an adolescent to believe he or she has gained control of someone or something thought to be out of control, hopeless, or disastrous; and (c) a **communication function**, which lets others know that something is wrong or that the adolescent is in emotional pain.

Often suicidal adolescents distort their thinking patterns in conjunction with the three functions of avoidance, control, and communication so that suicide becomes the best or only problem-solving option. Such distortions can take a number of directions. All-or-nothing thinking, for example, can enable an adolescent to believe that the only two options are continuing to be miserable and depressed or committing suicide; no problem-solving options may seem possible (Capuzzi, 1988). Identification of a single event, which is then applied to all events, is another cognitive distortion, over-generalization. Being left out of a party or trip to the mountains with friends may be used as "evidence" that the adolescent has no friends, that he or she is a "loser" or will always be forgotten or left out. "I can't seem to learn the material for this class very easily" becomes "I'm never going to make it through school" or "I'll probably have just as hard time when I start working full time." Adolescents who are experiencing stress and pain and who are becoming preoccupied with suicidal thoughts often experience an increasing number of cognitive distortions. Such distortions result in the adolescent becoming more and more negative and more and more supportive of one of the following motivations for carrying out a suicide plan:

- Wanting to escape from a situation that seems (or is) intolerable (e.g., sexual abuse, conflict with peers or teachers, pregnancy).
- Wanting to join someone who has died.
- Wanting to attract the attention of family or friends.
- Wanting to manipulate someone else.
- Wanting to avoid punishment.
- Wanting to be punished.
- Wanting to control when or how death will occur (an adolescent with a chronic or terminal illness may be motivated in this way).
- Wanting to end a conflict that seems unresolvable.
- Wanting to punish the survivors.
- Wanting revenge.

Personality Traits

As noted by Capuzzi (1988), it would be ideal if the research on suicidal adolescents provided practitioners with such a succinct profile of personality traits that teenagers at risk for suicide could be identified far in advance of any suicidal risk. Adolescents who fit the profile could then be assisted through individual and group counseling and other means. Although no consensus has yet been reached on the "usual," "typical," or "average" constellation of personality traits of the suicidal adolescent, researchers have agreed on a number of characteristics that seem to be common to many suicidal adolescents.

Low self-esteem. A number of studies have connected low self-esteem with suicide probability (Cull & Gill, 1982; Faigel, 1966; Stein & Davis, 1982; Stillion, McDowell, & Shamblin, 1984). My counseling experience, as well as the experience of other practitioners, seems to confirm the relationship between low self-esteem and suicide probability. Almost all such clients have issues focused on feelings of low self-worth and almost all such adolescents have experienced these self-doubts for an extended time period.

Hopelessness/helplessness. Most suicidal adolescents report feeling hopeless and helpless in relation to their circumstances as well as their ability to cope with these circumstances. The research support for verification of what clinicians report is growing (Cull & Gill, 1982; Jacobs, 1971; Kovacs, Beck, & Weissman, 1975; Peck, 1983). Most practitioners can expect to address this issue with suicidal clients and to identify a long-term history of feeling hopeless and helpless on the part of most clients.

Isolation. Many, if not most, suicidal adolescents tend to develop a small network of social support. They may find it difficult to make new friends, thus they rely on a small number of friends for support and companionship. (This may be why those around a suicide victim so often state that they did not notice anything unusual. The suicidal adolescent may not be in the habit of getting close enough to others for them to notice the changes in behavior, outlook, etc.) A number of authorities support this observation (Hafen, 1972; Kiev, 1977; Peck, 1983; Sommes, 1984; Stein & Davis, 1982).

High stress. High stress coupled with poor stress management skills seems to be characteristic of the suicidal adolescent. A number of studies have addressed this trait in terms of low frustration tolerance (Cantor, 1976; Kiev, 1977).

Acting out. Suicidal adolescents frequently evidence behaviors such as truancy, running away, refusal to cooperate at home or at school, use or abuse of alcohol or other drugs, and experimentation with sex. Such behaviors may be manifestations of depression. Often, adults remain so focused on the troublesome behavior connected with an adolescent's need to act out that the underlying depressive episodes may be overlooked.

Need to achieve. Sometimes, adolescents who are suicidal exhibit high achievement. This achievement may be focused on getting good grades, being the "class clown," accepting the most "dares," wearing the best clothes, or any of a number of other possibilities. In my counseling experience, this emphasis on achievement often is a compensation for feelings of low self-esteem. One should not jump to the conclusion that every adolescent who achieves at a high level is suicidal. This trait, along with all of the other traits and characteristics connected with the profile of the suicidal adolescent, must be assessed in the context of other observations.

Poor communication skills. Suicidal adolescents often have a history of difficulty in expressing thoughts and feelings. Such adolescents may have trouble identifying and labeling what they are feeling; self-expression seems awkward. It is not unusual to discover that adolescents who have become preoccupied with suicidal thoughts have experienced a series of losses or disappointments that they have never been able to discuss and, understandably, integrate or resolve.

Other directedness. Most suicidal adolescents are "other" rather than "inner" directed. They see themselves as what others have told them they are instead of what they want to be;

they value what others have said they "should be" instead of what they believe to be of personal value and worth. This trait may also be linked to low self-esteem and may lead to feelings of helplessness or inability to control interactions or circumstances around them.

Guilt. Usually connected with feelings of low self-esteem and a need to be other-directed, the guilt experienced by many suicidal adolescents is sometimes linked to "wanting to be punished." "Nothing I do seems to be good enough" or "I feel so bad because I disappointed them" or "I should not have made that decision; I should have known better" are statements common to the guilt-ridden suicidal adolescent.

Depression. Depression is a major element in the total profile of the suicidal adolescent. Hafen and Frandsen (1986) pointed out that there are sometimes differences between depression in an adult and depression in an adolescent. Adults are often despondent, tearful, sad, or incapable of functioning as usual. Although adolescents sometimes exhibit these characteristics, they may also respond with anger, rebelliousness, truancy, running away, using and abusing drugs, etc. Those adults and peers who associate depression only with feelings of sadness and despondency may not recognize depression in adolescents who mask it with behavior that disrupts the family and school environments.

Considering the complexity of the environment that adolescents must confront, it is normal for them to experience some short-term depression. But when depression becomes more frequent and more intense, to the point that the adolescent has trouble functioning at school or at home, it may indicate more serious problems.

Although contemporary literature often speaks of depression and suicide together, the link between the two is not yet clear. Empirically, there seems to be a strong link between depression and suicidal ideation because a high percentage of youth with suicidal ideation show signs of depression. However, the majority of depressed youth are not suicidal.

Often it is not the appearance of depression by itself that seems to correlate with suicidal behavior, but depression appearing with one or both of the following conditions, which then create a serious situation. Depression together with substance abuse is often found in the profile of completers. Berman and Jobes (1991) noted that the "wish to die" increases threefold with the onset of substance abuse.

Linked with both depression and substance abuse in suicidal behavior is conduct disorder. This personality disorder is characterized by antisocial behavior, including breaking laws and misbehaving in school. Shaffer and Gold (cited in Berman & Jobes, 1991) note a preponderance of antisocial behavior in completers.

It is extremely important for counselors and other professionals who may be working with suicidal adolescents to complete additional coursework or training experiences to learn about resources. Guidelines such as those provided by McWhirter and Kigin (1988) and the *Diagnostic and Statistical Manual of Mental Disorders—Revised* (American Psychiatric Association, 1987) are readily available to mental health practitioners; case supervision and consultation may also be needed to determine the nature of a depressive episode accurately. The DSM3-R, 1987, system of classifying depression is useful. There are three major sections as follows:

1. Major Affective Disorder
   a. Major Depression
   b. Bipolar Disorder

2. Other Specific Affective Disorder: At least two years' duration
    a. Cyclothymic Disorder (mild bipolar)
    b. Dysthymic Disorder

3. Atypical Affective Disorders: Those not categorized above
    a. Atypical Bipolar Disorder
    b. Atypical Depression

Frequently, well-meaning practitioners fail to discriminate between depression created by a constellation of factors (negative self-talk, poor problem solving skills, high stress) and depression that is endogenous and a result of the body chemistry inherited at birth. Treatment or counseling plans are different based on the kind of depression being experienced. Counselors, therapists, and core or crisis team members need to communicate with nurse-practitioners and psychiatrists when medical assessment and subsequent medication is appropriate for endogenous depression.

Internalizing Disorders in Children and Adolescents, by Reynolds (1992), provides an excellent overview of measures of depression for use with children or adolescents. The following instruments are described in detail. (NOTE: It may not be necessary to spend time on the following listings during an in-service session. They are included because faculty and staff usually ask about the specifics of assessing depression.)

1. **Children's Depression Inventory (CDI)**. This inventory has 27 items, each specific to a symptom of depression. Those tested select the symptom level that best describes what children are feeling. Several studies have been completed regarding use of the CDI to differentiate between depressed and nondepressed youth. Results for this use are mixed. CDI is used primarily to measure severity. The recommended cutoff score is 19 to designate a clinical level of depression. (Refer to the Reynolds [1992] text referenced above for details of validity and reliability.) The CDI is a useful self-report measure of the severity of depression in children. Some limitations exist, including lack of a test manual and normative information, and the guidelines for interpretation of scores present some difficulty.

2. **Reynolds Child Depression Scale (RCDS)**. A self-reporting 30-item format designed to identify symptoms of depression in youth age eight through 13. The child responds to the frequency of feelings (during the past two weeks) on a Likert scale.

3. **Children's Depression Scale (CDS)** (Lang & Tisher, 1978). A self-report and parent-report measure of children's depression. The time necessary for administration is similar to that of a clinical interview.

4. **Reynolds Adolescent Depression Scale (RADS)**. Designed to assess the severity of depressive symptoms in youth age 12 to 18. Responses are of a Likert type. Reading level is grade three. The RADS has a comprehensive manual covering validity, reliability, and interpretation of results. A cutoff score is recommended to reflect a clinically relevant level of symptom severity.

5. **Beck Depression Inventory (BDI)** (Beck, Ward, Mendelson, Mock, & Erbaugh, 1961). Designed for use with adults. Reading level and format cause difficulty for some adolescents. There is no determined cutoff point for adolescent use.

6. **Center for Epidemiological Studies—Depression Scale (CES-DS).** The scale is designed for use with adults and does not have a well-defined cutoff point for adolescent use.

In addition to self-reporting instruments, ratings by significant others often are used to determine the existence of depression as well as its severity. Instruments designed for significant other reporting are as follows:

1. **The Peer Nomination Inventory for Depression (PNID)** (Lefkowitz & Tesiny, 1980). A peer report instrument designed to assess depression in children. Useful as one component in a multimethod assessment of a child's depression.

2. **Personality Inventory for Children (PIC)** (Wirt, Lachar, Klinedinst, & Seat, 1977). A multidimensional assessment measure that includes a depression subscale and clinical scales.

3. **Child Behavior Checklists—Parent Form, Teacher Form, and Youth Self-Report (CBCL)** (Achenbach, 1983; Achenbach & Edelbrock, 1986, 1987). Three separate checklists and manuals. Self-report section is designed for ages 11 to 18.

One of the most common and most reliable tools for evaluating adolescent depression is the clinical interview. The interview allows the professional to probe and question and to make specific determinations about the status of the depression. The interview allows the professional to determine whether hallucinations are occurring. Limitations are ones of time and the necessity of having a trained examiner. Several semistructured interview forms have been designed to overcome the limitations mentioned.

1. **Bellevue Index of Depression (BID)** (Petti, 1983). Designed to assess depression in children age six to 12. Normal length of administration is 20 to 40 minutes. There are parent and child forms.

2. **Children's Depression Rating Scale—Revised (CDRS)** (Poznanski, Cook, & Carroll, 1979). Interview format to assess the severity of depression in children age eight to 12. Twenty to 30 minutes' duration.

3. **Hamilton Depression Rating Scale (HDRS).** Used successfully with adults; satisfactory reliability with adolescents.

4. **Diagnostic Interview Schedule for Children (DISC)** (Hamilton, 1967). Developed for use with adults. There are child and parent forms. The child form takes about 45 minutes; the parent form takes about 70 minutes to administer.

5. **Diagnostic Interview for Children and Adolescents (DICA)** (Herjanic & Reich, 1982). Research suggests good diagnostic utility.

Poor problem-solving skills. Most parents notice differences in the problem-solving ability of their children. Some children are more resourceful than others in identifying problem-resolution options. Suicidal adolescents seem to have less ability to develop solutions to troublesome situations or uncomfortable relationships. This may be one reason why suicidal preoccupation can progress from a cognitive focus to an applied plan with little consideration of other options.

HOW YOU CAN HELP

If you have concerns about an adolescent in your school, your role is to express your concern to the student, develop rapport, and facilitate a meeting with the school counselor or crisis team member. This meeting should take place as quickly as possible. Most adolescents attempt suicide 24 to 72 hours after their peak period of suicidal preoccupation.

The following guidelines may be helpful to you in getting a student to someone who can make an assessment and decide what needs to be done.

Step 1

Assess the suicidal risk factors using what you know about the "profile" of a suicidal adolescent.

Do not be afraid to ask directly if the person has entertained thoughts of suicide. Experience shows that harm is rarely done by asking about such thoughts at an appropriate time. In fact, the suicidal individual often welcomes the query and the opportunity to open up and discuss it. Remember, the more detailed an individual's thoughts and plans, the more serious the suicidal possibility. However, all suicidal thoughts should be taken seriously.

Step 2

Listen and paraphrase.

The most important thing for a person in distress is talking to someone who will listen and really hear what is being said. Paraphrase what you think the person is saying.

Step 3

Evaluate the seriousness of the young person's situation.

It is possible for an adolescent to be extremely upset but not suicidal or to appear mildly upset and yet still be suicidal. Try to understand the situation and circumstances and the meaning attached to these by the individual you are concerned about.

Step 4

Take every complaint and feeling the person expresses seriously.

Do not dismiss or discount the person's concerns. Let the person know that you understand his or her perspective but that you also may be able to see things in another way.

Step 5

Begin to broaden the person's perspective of his or her past and present situation.

Point out that depression often makes people see only some things (the negatives) and be temporarily unable to see other things (the positives). Elicit positive aspects of the person's past and present that are being ignored but that could be regained.

Step 6

Be positive in your outlook about the future.

Let the adolescent know that predictions of a hopeless future are only guesses, not facts. Contrast the finality of death with the uncertainty the future holds. Speculate on how the person's life would be different if just one or two changes could be made but do not attempt to argue or convince.

Step 7

Evaluate available resources.

Help the person to identify and mobilize resources that can lend support during the crisis. Suicidal persons often withdraw from available support just when they need it most. Let the person know that you will help in any way you can and that others can help also. Strong, stable supports are essential to a distressed individual.

Step 8

Accompany the student to the counselor or crisis team member.

Call on whomever is needed, depending upon the severity of the situation. Do not try to handle everything alone. Convey an attitude of firmness and self-assurance so that the person will think that you know what you are doing and that whatever is necessary and appropriate will be done to help.

UNDERSTANDING THE MYTHS

- Adolescents who talk about suicide never attempt suicide.

- Suicide happens with no warning.

- Adolescents from affluent families attempt or complete suicide more often than adolescents from poor families.

- Once an adolescent is suicidal, he or she is suicidal forever.

- If an adolescent attempts suicide and survives, he or she will never make an additional attempt.

UNDERSTANDING THE MYTHS

- Adolescents who attempt or complete suicide always leave notes.

- Most adolescent suicides happen late at night or during the predawn hours.

- Never use the word suicide when talking to adolescents, because using the word gives some adolescents the idea.

- Every adolescent who attempts suicide is depressed.

- Suicide is hereditary.

RECOGNIZING THE PROFILE
(BEHAVIORS)

- Lack of concern about personal welfare.

- Changes in social patterns.

- A decline in school achievement.

- Difficulty in concentrating.

- Altered sleeping and eating patterns.

RECOGNIZING THE PROFILE
(BEHAVIORS)

- Attempts to put personal affairs in order or to make amends.

- Use or abuse of alcohol or drugs.

- Unusual interest in how others are feeling.

- Preoccupation with death and violence themes.

- Sudden improvement after a period of depression.

- Sudden or increased promiscuity.

RECOGNIZING THE PROFILE
(VERBAL CUES)

- No "universal" language for communicating suicidal intentions.

- Ask for clarification of what you hear:

  "Could you say a little more about what you mean when you say . . ."

- Paraphrase to communicate that you listened and to check accuracy:

  "You are really discouraged and upset about . . ."

RECOGNIZING THE PROFILE
(VERBAL CUES)

- "You won't be seeing me for my appointment on Monday."

- "I'm going home."

- "I thought about something I'm afraid to tell anyone about."

- "I'm tired."

- "I wonder what death is like."

- "She'll be sorry about how she treated me."

RECOGNIZING THE PROFILE
(THINKING PATTERNS AND MOTIVATIONS)

Motivations of suicidal adolescents can be understood more readily when suicide is viewed as fulfilling one of three primary functions:

- **Avoidance**

- **Control**

- **Communication**

RECOGNIZING THE PROFILE
(THINKING PATTERNS AND MOTIVATIONS)

- Wanting to escape an intolerable situation.

- Wanting to join someone who has died.

- Wanting to attract the attention of family or friends.

- Wanting to manipulate someone else.

- Wanting to avoid punishment.

RECOGNIZING THE PROFILE
(THINKING PATTERNS AND MOTIVATIONS)

- Wanting to be punished.

- Wanting to control when or how death will occur.

- Wanting to end a conflict.

- Wanting to punish the survivors.

- Wanting revenge.

RECOGNIZING THE PROFILE
(PERSONALITY TRAITS)

- **Low self-esteem**

- **Hopelessness/helplessness**

- **Isolation**

- **High stress**

- **Acting out**

- **Need to achieve**

RECOGNIZING THE PROFILE
(PERSONALITY TRAITS)

- Poor communication skills

- Other-directedness

- Guilt

- Depression

- Poor problem-solving skills

ADOLESCENT BEHAVIOR THAT MAY BE SYMPTOMATIC OF DEPRESSION

MASKED ADOLESCENT SYMPTOMS

- **Reckless behavior**

- **Boredom, lethargy**

- **Promiscuity**

- **Running away**

- **Defiance**

- **Truancy**

- **Antisocial behavior**

- **Drug or alcohol abuse**

- **Complaints of illness**

HOW YOU CAN HELP

- **Assess the suicidal risk.**

- **Listen and paraphrase.**

- **Evaluate the seriousness of the young person's situation.**

- **Take every complaint and feeling the person expresses seriously.**

- **Begin to broaden the person's perspective of his or her past and present situation.**

- **Be positive in your outlook about the future.**

- **Evaluate available resources.**

- **Accompany the student to the counselor or crisis team member.**

CHAPTER FOUR
PREPARATION OF CRISIS TEAMS

As the number of suicide attempts and completions rises, even the smallest school districts eventually will find themselves dealing with a crisis situation. The purpose of this chapter is to offer some suggestions to schools and school districts for handling crisis situations when they do occur. Waiting until the situation occurs will be too late. The seriousness of the suicidal situation requires plans that have already have been formulated so that they can be set into motion.

One of the most effective public school approaches to a suicide attempt or completion is formation of a crisis team. The team consists of trained staff from throughout the district who are able to offer consultation services, or in some cases, direct on-site service with parents, families, staff, and students. (In some schools these may be called student assitance teams, student services teams, or something similar.)

Crisis team building is unique for each district. It is important to follow the policy guidelines previously adopted by the school district. Referral recommendations also will be unique to the area as will media communications and within-district notifications. For these reasons, each district should form its own crisis plan.

In most cases, a district crisis team is formed to plan training exercises for district-wide team members. Often, each individual building has a crisis team representative who identifies individual team members from the representatives building. The role of a district crisis team member is always one of consultation or support; a member should never tell others what they should do in their own building.

Crisis teams need the same training or staff development that all faculty and staff receive, as described in the previous chapter. In addition, crisis teams need to be prepared in crisis management and postvention.

CRISIS MANAGEMENT

If an adolescent has been identified as potentially suicidal, every possible step should be taken to involve the adolescent in ongoing counseling so that preventive steps can be taken quickly. A number of cognitive/behavioral models have proven effective with depressed, suicidal adolescents. Ellis (1979), Krumboltz and Thoresen (1976), and Lazarus (1976) present frameworks for counselors to use with such adolescents. Numerous films, filmstrips, and videos are available for classroom guidance presentations (*Kidsrights Catalog*, 1993). In addition, the American Association of Suicidology's journal, *The Journal of Suicide and Life Threatening Behavior*, is an excellent resource for professionals.

There are times, however, when adolescents at risk for suicide are not identified until a crisis state has been reached. In such circumstances, it is important for all concerned to initiate action to assess lethality and determine appropriate follow-up. Since many professionals who are not counselors lack experience with adolescents who are in the midst of a personal crisis, the following guidelines may prove helpful:

1. **Remember the meaning of the term "crisis management."** When thinking of crisis management, it is important to understand the meaning of the word "crisis" as well as the word "management." The word "crisis" means that the situation is not usual, normal, or average; a suicidal adolescent is highly stressed and in considerable emotional discomfort. Adolescents in crisis usually feel vulnerable, hopeless, angry, low in self-esteem, and at a loss as to how to cope. The word "management" means that the professional involved must be prepared to apply skills that are different from those required for preventive or postvention counseling. An adolescent in crisis must be assessed, directed, monitored, and guided to prevent a self-destructive act. Since adolescents experiencing a suicidal crisis may be quite volatile and impulsive, the need for decisive, rapid decision making by the intervener is extremely important.

2. **Be calm and supportive.** An intervener's calm, supportive manner conveys respect for the perceptions and internal pain of a suicidal adolescent. Remember that such adolescents usually feel hopeless and highly stressed. **The demeanor and attitude of the helping person is pivotal in the process of offering assistance.**

3. **Be nonjudgmental.** Statements such as, "You can't be thinking of suicide; it is against the teachings of your church" or "I had a similar problem when I was your age and I didn't consider suicide" are totally inappropriate during a crisis situation. An adolescent's perception of a situation must be respected. The same caution can be applied to the necessity of respecting a suicidal adolescent's expression of feelings whether these feelings are of depression, frustration, fear, or helplessness. Judgmental, unaccepting responses and comments only serve to damage an already impaired sense of self-esteem further and decrease willingness to communicate. Adolescents could sink further into depression or increase their resolve to carry through with a suicide plan if others are critical and unwilling to acknowledge what appear, to the adolescent, to be insurmountable obstacles.

4. **Encourage self-disclosure.** The very act of talking about painful emotions and difficult circumstances is the first step in what can become a long-term healing process. A professional helper may be the first person with whom a suicidal adolescent has shared and trusted in months or even years and it may be difficult for the adolescent simply because he or she is not used to communicating thoughts and feelings. It is important to keep the suicidal adolescent talking about his or her feelings so that the adolescent's seriousness of intentions can be determined early in the intervention process.

5. **Acknowledge the reality of suicide as a choice, but do not "normalize" suicide as a choice.** Practitioners should let adolescents know that they are not alone and isolated with respect to suicidal preoccupation. It is also important to communicate the idea that suicide is a choice, a problem-solving option, and that other choices and options are available. This may be difficult to do in a way that does not make

such an adolescent feel "judged" or "put down." "It's not unusual for adolescents to be so upset with relationships or circumstances that thoughts of suicide occur more and more frequently; this doesn't mean that you're weird or a freak. I'm really glad you've chosen to talk to me about how you're feeling and what you're thinking. You've made a good choice since now you can begin exploring other ways to solve the problems you described" is an example of what could be said to an adolescent in crisis.

6. **Listen actively and reinforce positively.** During the initial stages of the crisis management process, it is important to let the adolescent at risk for suicide know you are listening carefully and really understanding how difficult life has been. Not only will such careful listening and communicating on the part of the professional make it easier for the adolescent to share, but it also will provide the basis for a growing sense of self-respect. Being listened to, heard, and respected is a powerful and empowering experience for anyone who is at a loss about how to cope.

7. **Do not attempt in-depth counseling.** Although it is very important for a suicidal adolescent to begin to overcome feelings of despair and to develop a sense of control as soon as possible, the emotional turmoil and stress experienced during a crisis usually makes in-depth counseling impossible. Developing a plan to begin ameliorating the sense of crisis an adolescent may be experiencing is extremely important, however, and should be accomplished as quickly as possible. Crisis management necessitates developing a plan to lessen the crisis; this plan should be shared with the adolescent so that it is clear that his or her circumstances will improve. **Counseling/therapy cannot really take place during the height of a suicidal crisis.**

8. **Contact another professional.** It is a good idea to enlist the assistance of another professional, trained in crisis management, when an adolescent thought to be at risk for suicide is brought to your attention. School and mental health counselors should ask a colleague to assist with assessment. It is always a good idea to have the support of a colleague who understands the dynamics of a suicidal crisis; in addition, the observations made by two professionals are more likely to be more comprehensive. Since suicidal adolescents may present a situation that, if misjudged or mismanaged, could result in a subsequent attempt or completion, it is in the best interests of both the professional and the client for professionals to work collaboratively whenever possible. It also should be noted that liability questions are less likely to become issues and professional judgment is less likely to be questioned if the severity of a suicidal crisis and associated recommendations for crisis management have been assessed on a collaborative basis.

9. **Ask questions to assess lethality.** A number of dimensions must be explored to assess lethality. This assessment can be accomplished through an interview format (**a crisis situation is not conducive to administration of a written appraisal instrument**). The following questions (which, with the exception of the first one asked first, need not be asked in order) help determine the degree of risk in a suicidal crisis; all of them do not need to be asked if the interview results in spontaneous disclosure of the information:

    "What has happened to make life so difficult?" The more an adolescent describes the circumstances that have contributed to feelings of despair and hopelessness, the better the opportunity for effective crisis management. The process of talking about stress-producing interpersonal situations and circum-

stances may begin to lower the adolescent's feelings of stress and reduce risk. It is not unusual for an adolescent in the midst of a suicidal crisis to describe a multifaceted set of problems involving family, peers, school, and drugs. The more problems an adolescent describes as stress-producing, and the more complicated the scenario, the higher the lethality or risk.

"Are you thinking of suicide?" Adolescents who have been preoccupied with suicidal thoughts may experience a sense of relief to know that someone is able to discuss suicide in a straightforward manner. Using the word "suicide" will convey that the helping professional is listening and is willing to be involved; using the word "suicide" will not put the idea of suicide in the mind of a nonsuicidal adolescent.

"How long have you been thinking about suicide?" Adolescents who have been preoccupied with suicide for a period of several weeks are more lethal than those who have considered it only fleetingly. One way to explore several components of this question is to remember the acronym "FID." When asking about suicidal thoughts, ask about *frequency* or how often they occur, *intensity* or how dysfunctional the preoccupation is making the adolescent ("Can you go on with your daily routine as usual?"), and *duration* or how long the periods of preoccupation last. Obviously, an adolescent who reports frequent periods of preoccupation so intense that it is difficult or impossible to go to school, to work, or to see friends, and for increasingly longer periods of time so that periods of preoccupation and dysfunction are merging, is more lethal than an adolescent who describes a different set of circumstances.

"Do you have a suicide plan?" When an adolescent is able to be specific about the method, the time, the place, and who will or will not be nearby, the risk is higher. (If the use of a gun, knife, medication, or other means is described, ask if that item is in a pocket or purse and request that the item be left with you. Never, however, enter into a struggle with an adolescent to remove a firearm. Call the police or local suicide or crisis center.) Most adolescents will cooperate with you by telling you about the plan and allowing you to separate them from the means. Remember, most suicidal adolescents are other-directed; such a trait should be taken advantage of during a crisis-management situation. Later, when the crisis has subsided and counseling is initiated, the adolescent's internal locus of control can be strengthened.

"Do you know someone who has committed suicide?" If the answer is yes, the adolescent may be at higher risk, especially if this incident occurred within the family or a close network of friends. Such an adolescent may have come to believe that suicide is a legitimate problem-solving option.

"How much do you want to live?" An adolescent who can provide only a few reasons for wishing to live is at higher risk than an adolescent who can enumerate a number of reasons.

"How much do you want to die?" The response to this question provides the opposite view of the one above. An adolescent who gives a variety of reasons for wishing to die is more lethal than an adolescent who cannot provide justification for ending life. It may be unnecessary to ask this question if the answer to the previous question provided enough information.

"What do you think death is like?" This question can be an excellent tool for assessment purposes. Adolescents who do not seem to realize that death is permanent, that no reversal is possible, and that they cannot physically return are at higher risk for an actual attempt. Also, adolescents who have the idea that death will be "romantic," "nurturing," or "the solution to current problems" are at high risk.

"Have you attempted suicide in the past?" If the answer to this question is yes, the adolescent is more lethal. Another, successful attempt could be made because a previous attempter remembers earlier efforts and the fact that he or she thought up and carried through a suicide plan. The second attempt might correct deficits in the original plan and result in death.

"How long ago was this previous attempt?" should be asked of any adolescent who answers yes to the previous question. The more recent the previous attempt, the more lethal the adolescent and the more critical the crisis management process.

"Have you been feeling depressed?" Since a high percentage of adolescents who attempt or complete suicide are depressed, this is an important question. Using the acronym FID to remember to ask about frequency, intensity, and duration is also helpful in the context of exploring an adolescent's response to this question. As previously discussed, a determination needs to be made about whether the adolescent is clinically depressed. Adolescents who report frequent, intense, and lengthy periods of depression resulting in dysfunctional episodes that are occurring closer and closer together, or are happening continuously, are at high risk.

"Is there anyone to stop you?" This is an extremely important question. If an adolescent has a difficult time identifying a friend, family member, or significant adult who is worth living for, the probability of a suicide attempt is high. Whomever the adolescent can identify should be specifically named; addresses, phone numbers, and the relationship to the adolescent also should be obtained. (If the adolescent cannot remember phone numbers and addresses, look up the information, together, in a phone book.) In the event it is decided that a suicide watch should be initiated, the people in the adolescent's network can be contacted and asked to participate.

"On a scale of one to 10, with one being low and 10 being high, what number depicts the probability that you will attempt suicide?" The higher the number, the higher the lethality.

"Do you use alcohol or other drugs?" If the answer to this question is yes, the lethality is higher because use of a substance further distorts cognition and weakens impulse control. A yes answer also should be followed by an exploration of the degree of drug involvement and identification of specific drugs.

"Have you experienced significant losses during the past year or earlier losses you've never discussed?" Adolescents who have lost friends because of moving, vitality because of illness, their family because of a divorce, etc., are vulnerable to stress and confusion and are usually at higher risk for attempting or completing suicide if they have been preoccupied with such thoughts.

"Have you been concerned, in any way, with your sexuality?" This may be a difficult question to explore, even briefly, during a peaking suicidal crisis. Generally, adolescents who are, or think they may be, gay or lesbian are at higher risk for suicide. It is quite difficult for adolescents to deal with the issue of sexual orientation because they fear being ridiculed or rejected. They may have experienced related guilt and stress for a number of years, never daring to discuss their feelings with anyone.

"When you think about yourself and the future, what do you visualize?" A high-risk adolescent probably will have difficulty visualizing the future and will describe feeling too hopeless and depressed to even imagine a future life.

As noted at the beginning of this discussion, it is not necessary to ask all of these questions if their answers are shared during the course of the discussion. It should also be noted that the interviewing team must make judgments about the truthfulness of a specific response by considering each response in the total context of the interview.

10. **Make crisis-management decisions.** If as a result of an assessment made by at least two professionals, the adolescent is at risk for suicide, a number of crisis-management interventions can be considered. They may be used singly or in combination; the actual combination will depend on the lethality determination, resources and people available, and professional judgment. The professionals involved, however, are responsible for developing a crisis-management plan to be followed until the crisis subsides and long-term counseling or therapy can be initiated.

Notification of parents. Parents of minors must be notified and asked for assistance when an adolescent is determined to be at risk for suicide. Often, adolescents may ask a school or mental health counselor who learns about suicidal intent not to tell anyone. **Such confidentiality is not possible; the welfare of the adolescent is the most important consideration and parents should be contacted as soon as possible.**

Sometimes parents do not believe that their child is suicidal and refuse to leave home or work and meet with their son or daughter and members of the crisis team. At times parents may be adamant in their demands that the school or mental health professional withdraw their involvement. Although such attitudes are not conducive to the management of a suicidal crisis, they are understandable since parents may respond with denial or anger to mask how they really feel, especially if they believe their own inadequacies as parents are at fault. Because a suicidal adolescent cannot be left unmonitored, this provides a dilemma for a school. **Since conforming to the wishes of uncooperative parents places the adolescent at even greater risk, steps must be taken despite parental protests.** Although some professionals worry about liability issues in such circumstances, liability is higher if such an adolescent is allowed to leave unmonitored and with no provision for follow-up assistance. **Schools should confer with legal counsel to understand liability issues and to insure that the best practices are followed in such circumstances.**

Considering hospitalization. Hospitalization can be the option of choice during a suicidal crisis (even if the parents are cooperating) when the risk is high. An adolescent who has not been sleeping or eating, for example, may be totally exhausted or highly agitated. The care and safety that can be offered in a psychiatric unit of a hospital is often needed until the adolescent can feel less stressed, obtain food and rest, and realize that others consider the circumstances painful and worthy of attention. In many hospital settings, multidisciplinary teams (physicians, psychiatrists, counselors, social workers, nurses, nurse-practitioners, teachers) work to individualize a treatment plan and provide for outpatient help as soon as the need for inpatient assistance subsides.

Writing contracts. Professionals may decide that developing a contract with the adolescent may be enough to support the adolescent through the crisis period and into a more positive frame of mind after which he or she would be more receptive to long-term counseling or therapy. Such a contract should be written, signed, and dated by the adolescent and the counselor. The contract also can be witnessed and signed by other professionals, friends, or family members.

Contracts should require the adolescent to:

1. agree not to attempt suicide;
2. get enough food and sleep;
3. discard items that could be used in a suicide attempt (guns, weapons, medications, etc.);
4. specify the time span of the contract;
5. call a counselor, Crisis Center, etc., if he or she is tempted to break the contract or attempt suicide,
6. write down the phone numbers of people to contact if the feeling of crisis escalates; and
7. specify ways time will be structured (walks, talks, movies, etc.).

Organizing suicide watches. If hospital psychiatric services on an inpatient basis are not available in a given community and those doing the assessment believe the suicide risk is high, a suicide watch should be organized by contacting the individuals whom the adolescent has identified in response to the question, "Is there anyone to stop you?" After receiving the professional's instruction and orientation, family members and friends should take turns staying with the adolescent until the crisis has subsided and long-term counseling or therapy has begun. It is never a good idea to depend on a family member to carry out a suicide watch alone; it is usually too difficult for family members to retain perspective. Friends should be included in a suicide watch, even though confidentiality, as discussed earlier, cannot be maintained.

POSTVENTION

When an adolescent has attempted or completed a suicide, it is imperative, particularly in a school setting, to be aware of the impact of such an event on the "system." Usually, within just a few hours, the peer group finds out that an adolescent has attempted or completed suicide. This could present a problem to the faculty and staff in a given school building since not answering questions raised by students can engender misinformation or rumors. The guidelines presented in this section are adapted from those developed by the American Association of Suicidology (1987).

For schools to deal effectively with the impact of a student's or faculty member's suicide, they need a postvention plan to guide their actions. The impact of a suicide is devastating and includes fear, panic, anger, sorrow, and other signs of grief. There is a real danger that other vulnerable young people will choose to imitate the suicide act. Although the dynamics of contagion are not fully understood, cluster suicides are a reality. The school and the community must work together to provide reassurance and a better sense of security after a suicide. Timely and appropriate efforts can alleviate the intensity of the crisis, help protect other at-risk students, and facilitate the recovery process. Such a plan should be established before a suicide, not after.

No model postvention plan will fit every community and school district or even every school within a school district. Each institution has its own organization, traditions, and resources. No two suicides will have exactly the same impact. The circumstances of the suicide, the relationship of the victim to the survivors, and the context in which it takes place, all serve to make each one unique. All those associated with the victims become, in effect, survivors of the tragedy and are subject to a predictable range of emotional responses. Such reactions can affect institutions, organizations, and, in some situations, entire communities. Because such reactions can be anticipated, responses should be planned in advance.

The suggestions that follow offer guidelines to help schools and their communities as they undertake the process of creating their own postvention policies and procedures. The school/community plan must be developed *before* a successful youth suicide or, in some cases, a suicide attempt.

GOALS

1. **To help the students, faculty, and support staff with the grieving process.** Above all, the crisis team needs to be compassionate and mindful of the emotional pain experienced by survivors of suicide. When proper guidance is provided, coping skills can be strengthened by loss. (Friends of the suicide victim may grieve while others may exhibit other reactions to the trauma.) Screening should be done during postvention to determine who shows signs of extreme emotional distress and needs psychological assistance. Suicide survivorship can precipitate many psychological or psychiatric conditions, including post-traumatic stress disorder, depression, separation anxiety, substance abuse, and school failure. Postvention provides the opportunity to introduce additional resources and assistance. The initial hours and days following a suicide are critical for the grieving survivors to begin the difficult journey of emotional healing.

2. **To prevent further suicides.** It has been well documented that vulnerable teenagers may imitate a suicide of a classmate, acquaintance, or anyone with whom they identify. Contagion is a real danger.

CRISIS TEAM: MANAGING THE CRISIS

The first step in developing a school postvention plan is to designate a crisis team leader who has decision-making authority to coordinate assignments and communicate with the building administrator. The team is responsible for overall implementation of the plan. Its members should be trained in grief counseling and crisis intervention. At least some of the crisis team members need to have prior firsthand experience with a postvention. This assignment takes priority over other job assignments so that the team can convene quickly, within an hour or two of being called.

As noted earlier, crisis team members should be selected from the school and/or school district. Team members can be drawn from the ranks of guidance counselors, nurses, psychologists, social workers, and other staff with similar training in crisis situations. Supplemental training may be needed in suicide assessment, crisis management, grief counseling, and postvention principles. Experienced staff from other schools or a central office can be called upon to assist. At least one person on the crisis team who is not emotionally involved with the deceased student and the school supervisors should be assigned to the building. It may be useful to bring in someone to assist in organizing and record keeping.

Schools also may find it helpful to use an outside consultant to provide guidance to the crisis team and the school administration. These experienced and knowledgeable professionals bring a greater objectivity to these intensely emotional situations. However, even when a consultant is available, the brunt of postvention activities will fall on the school staff. The school crisis team and school personnel need to be empowered to take the lead in the postvention process, with the consultant playing a supportive role.

The size of the crisis team will depend on available resources, the size of the school, and the impact of the suicide. Six members is a suggested minimum to meet immediately after the suicide. The team's size may be increased or decreased, according to need. Counselors and staff from other schools are a logical adjunct resource.

The team members should meet before implementing the postvention plan, several times during the day in the early stages to review or revise the assignments, and at the end of each day to debrief, process, and support each other. Postvention work is stressful. Team members need to know this and plan ways to insure mutual support as well as support to the school principal. The team and its leader must maintain a link with the school principal and central school administration during the entire course of the postvention. (It is advisable for the team leader to be responsible for seeing that careful records and documentation are kept of all at-risk students who are identified or referred for counseling.)

DISSEMINATING INFORMATION

Immediately after a suicide, one of the first issues is how to best tell students and faculty. The death must be addressed openly and directly. Once the basic facts of a suicide are known, any attempt to delay informing the students will only encourage rumors. There is no way to keep the suicide of a student or teacher secret, even if the family requests it. How this information is passed on is very important. Most survivors can remember years later how they first learned of the suicide and negative effects are evident if the information was not presented honestly and with empathy.

The following steps need to be taken:

1. **Verify the information from police and/or medical examiner.** When the issue of whether a death is a suicide has not been determined yet, questions can be dealt with by acknowledging this uncertainty and using the term "apparent" suicide.

2. **Tell the faculty first, ideally at a meeting or by a chain telephone call before the beginning of classes.** (Most schools have an existing mechanism for disseminating important information quickly.) Remember that the faculty are as much survivors as the students and also will be having intense reactions. Help them anticipate their students' reactions and questions and be alert for anyone needing additional

attention. If a meeting cannot be called for the faculty, have members of the crisis team go to each classroom individually to inform the teachers. Make plans to notify the support staff or others who are unable to attend the meeting.

3. **Call close friends out of class to tell them individually.** It helps for both faculty and students to learn of the death from a familiar person first.

4. **Prepare a brief written statement; have members of the crisis team or another teacher pair up to talk to the class together.** This statement should include the basic facts of the suicide without disclosing the precise description and details of the method, a recognition of the sorrow and distress the news will cause, and information about the resources that will be available to help students with their grief. Avoid the use of a loudspeaker or large assemblies to disseminate this information. If the school intercom is used, the announcement should be followed by class discussions to allow an opportunity to share feelings in a small group setting.

5. **Communicate this information to the central administration and other schools in the district that may have siblings or friends affected by the death.** This promotes the two-way exchange of information and resources.

6. **Send a letter with correct information to classmates' parents or provide some way to inform parents.** This is necessary to tell parents the real situation and to alert them to be sensitive to their child's reactions to the tragedy. The letter should encourage families to come to the school with any personal concerns and to report any changes in their children's behavior. Instruct the school secretary or receptionist how to handle telephone calls from parents and requests for information from the media or other community members. This promotes two-way communication by providing information and welcoming helpful ideas.

PROVISION FOR INDIVIDUAL AND GROUP COUNSELING

In the days immediately after a suicide, two things should be going on simultaneously: a calm, supportive atmosphere should be maintained, and special counseling initiatives should be provided. For many students, the predictability of the school routine is reassuring during a time of stress. The school should remain open and maintain, as far as possible, its normal schedule. Some reduction in activities is indicated; tests should be rescheduled if at all possible. At the same time, a flexible approach should be adopted that provides maximum opportunity to students to talk about their feelings. Besides encouraging use of existing counseling resources, the school will need to initiate special outreach and screening measures.

Careful selection of counseling rooms is one of the first decisions to be made. Preparation for counseling should be made at the same time information is being disseminated. The rooms must be appropriate for groups as well as individual counseling. Pick private places, free from interruption and conducive to the counseling process. A home economics living room, a corner of the library, or a counselor's meeting room works well. The cafeteria or auditorium do not lend themselves to individual or group counseling. Using a large room filled with a number of students could cause emotional contagion.

Some students will require special screening either because they were close friends or relatives of the victim, or because they constitute an at-risk group. Students with a record of suicidal behavior, an association with someone else who committed suicide, or with known histories of depression or other emotional illness should be seen individually. The suicide may also affect students deeply who have suffered the recent loss of someone close. If possible, these students should be seen by their own school counselor or a school psychologist who has worked with them before.

The closer the relationship, the more intense the survivor's reaction is likely to be. It is also possible that some friends may feel guilt because they had some advance warning of the suicide. A group counseling approach can be especially appropriate with friends because of the commonality of their reactions. A group experience can help them learn how to support each other. Undoubtedly they will be spending time together outside of the group and outside of school. In general, it will not be possible to anticipate who will be seriously upset or endangered by the suicide. Those with no obvious connection to the victim can still be at risk and should have the opportunity to identify themselves or be referred for counseling. Students who may be at increased risk because of the suicide include those who:

1. have a history of previous suicide attempts;
2. experience emotional difficulties;
3. have been hospitalized for emotional problems or drug or alcohol rehabilitation;
4. had a close relationship with the deceased (real or imagined);
5. might identify with the deceased or see the deceased as a role model;
6. are preoccupied with death or suicide;
7. have experienced the recent death of a loved one;
8. have a personal history that includes the suicide of a family member or friend;
9. are friends or siblings of the deceased; or
10. self-identify as "at risk."

The key, therefore, is flexible and alert responsiveness by the crisis team to address concerns from a wide variety of sources. For this reason, the team size may have to be increased once these students are identified.

One or more crisis team members should be assigned to follow the victim's class schedule and assist the teachers in discussing the death. All should be encouraged to express their feelings and ask questions. Misconceptions about this suicide and suicide in general should be clarified, but it is not appropriate to turn the discussion into a lecture or formal lesson about suicide. Students can make plans to extend sympathy to the family or attend the funeral. Allow the students to participate in deciding what to do about the victim's empty desk. The teacher or administrator will assist the family in bringing home personal belongings.

The postvention counseling approach focuses on reactions that interfere with a healthy grieving process and with survivors' ability to cope with the crisis. It emphasizes validating and normalizing many conflicting reactions—i.e., anger, guilt, shame, blame, denial, and anxiety. While the timing and intensity of such reactions varies greatly, all survivors are vulnerable. Feelings of guilt are often paramount. A constant postvention theme is the basic reality that the suicide is an individual act by an individual, caused by a complex set of circumstances, for which others cannot assume responsibility. Grief resolution after suicide may take as long as two years. While intensive postvention efforts may close after a few weeks, a need for counseling may continue. The anniversary of the suicide and other special occasions may rekindle initial acute grief. The following interventions can prove useful in counseling survivors individually and in support groups.

Guidelines for Counseling

1. **Explain, encourage, and normalize expression of feelings such as shock, fear, sadness, guilt, anger at others or at the victim, etc.** Assure students that these painful feelings can and will be alleviated through discussion, counseling, and emotional support.

2. **Reassure that there is no "right way" to feel after a suicide.** Do not expect resolution of sorrow as a goal for the group or try to "cheer them up." They will need to experience the pain to progress through their grief.

3. **Help clarify the facts of the suicide.** Ask the students to repeat information they know and correct any errors.

4. **Encourage reality testing of the common misconception that someone other than the victim is to blame for the suicide.** The suicide was the victim's choice. The facilitator should not speculate why the victim chose to die or who is to blame. Acknowledge the desire to know why but point out that the only one who really knows the answer is dead.

5. **Do not describe the suicide in positive terms or glamorize the act.** Suicide is neither romantic nor heroic. It does bring attention, which may be appealing for those seeking it. The focus needs to be on ways to get attention from significant others without threatening or attempting suicide.

6. **Ask the students or survivors to relate memories about their friend.** These memories may be happy, sad, or angry. They can talk about how long they had known the victim, what they did together, what he or she was like, etc. Ask them to describe the last time they saw the victim and what they said or wish they had said if they had known this was to be the last time they saw the victim.

7. **Encourage discussion of recent losses and description of their experiences at funerals and what might be expected at this one.**

8. **Acknowledge that suicidal thoughts are common but do not have to be acted on.** Other alternatives and options are available.

9. **Rehearse possible condolence messages to the family.** This may be a new experience and students may be anxious because they do not know what to say.

10. **Encourage the students to talk to their parents and friends about their feelings and thoughts regarding the suicide.** Ask them to discuss positive experiences with help seeking. To whom do they turn for support?

11. **Direct students to available sources of assistance for themselves and their friends.** Be sure they know how to use the local hot line. Write down the telephone numbers of appropriate community resources. Check with each student to see if he or she is thinking about suicide. Be alert for these students who may need additional outside counseling when suicidal ideation is present and meet with the parents to make a referral.

Special initiatives are required to help school staff members as well. They, too, are survivors and in some cases their reactions may be even more intense than the students'. While they are dealing with their own reactions, they also are called upon to help their students through the crisis and to model appropriate responses. Crisis team members need to be available to meet the staff in small groups. Assigning a team member to the teachers' lounge and lunchroom can help facilitate discussion. A consultant or team member may wish to meet with the entire school staff to discuss how people react to suicide. Small group follow-up will be helpful for some. However, staff should be able to choose their own particular way of coping. Some of them will prefer to avoid all discussion of their own feelings and focus on the students. Their wishes need to be respected as long as they seem appropriate.

Release grieving students from school only with their parents' knowledge and approval. Do not permit students to leave the school building to go home to an empty house. They are much better off being with their friends and caring adults. If they prefer not to attend class, provide a place for them to be together or alone with a staff or crisis team member close by. People grieve in different ways. As long as it is not destructive, allow them to choose the place they find most comfortable.

Be attuned to the needs of friends and siblings at other schools. A member of the crisis team may need to be assigned to track them down and counsel them. Be sure to notify the principal of the elementary school or middle school that a high school suicide victim attended. Word usually spreads quickly, so they need to have accurate information too.

MEMORIALS AND THE FUNERAL

A balance needs to be maintained between supporting the grieving process and not glamorizing or sensationalizing the suicide. Maintaining this balance is a particularly delicate issue as the school decides on appropriate commemorative activities. Often the school custom with regard to student deaths will provide a baseline for the decision. Memorial activities should not go beyond what is customary in other situations. For example, if it is the custom to fly the flag at half-mast or have a moment of silent prayer, then this activity is all right.

Some memorial activities are questionable, even if they are customary. Do not dedicate an athletic event or other school activity to the deceased student. Establishing any kind of permanent memorial such as a plaque, planting a tree, dedicating the yearbook, or establishing a scholarship fund can become a constant invitation to consider suicide. Memorial assemblies can be too intense and difficult to manage. Grieving students may be very persistent in their efforts to honor the memory of the deceased friend. School personnel should understand and explain these responses as part of the grief process and channel the students' energies into constructive projects to help the living. If funds are collected they may be offered to the family to help with funeral expenses or donated to a community agency such as a crisis center.

All students wishing to attend the funeral service should be encouraged to do so, with the permission of their parents. Funerals play an important role in helping people to accept the reality of death. They provide rituals for the shared experience of grief. Encourage parents to accompany their children and to discuss the experience with them. Many students will be anxious about the funeral; preparing for its emotional impact can be a topic for individual and group counseling. The school or the teachers should not assume responsibility for taking students to the funeral home, church, or cemetery. A funeral service held after regular school hours minimizes the disruption of the regular school schedule. If this is not the choice of the family and the funeral is held during school hours, the school should stay open for those students who want to attend classes. If possible, provision also should be made for teachers to attend.

THE BEREAVED FAMILY

It is appropriate for the principal, counseling staff, and other faculty who had a close relationship with the victim to visit the bereaved family. The visit is an opportunity to offer condolences and support and to get accurate information or messages the family may wish to have passed on to their child's friends. It is not necessary, but it is helpful, if the parents would give their permission for disseminating information. If they refuse, the school is still faced with carrying out its crisis plan to help grieving survivors and prevent further suicidal activity. This puts the crisis team and the school administration in a difficult position.

The family can assist in identifying friends and siblings in other schools who may need assistance. Families often feel isolated and stigmatized. They need reassurance that they are not to blame. They may take comfort in knowing that the school is helping the other students and teachers with their grief and will often want to cooperate in this process. The family needs to know about the school's postvention efforts. It can be a time to help retrieve their child's belongings from school. They may wish to have the opportunity to do this in privacy or have someone else do it for them. The family also should be consulted about any planned memorial activity.

Meeting with the family also offers a chance to refer them to community agencies or survivor groups for support.

PARENTS

It will also be necessary to respond to the concerns of other students' parents and family members. They will be concerned about the welfare of their own children and will need reassurance and information. The school administration needs to be prepared to meet with concerned parents individually and in small groups and may want to reserve a block of time for this.

After the initial phases of the crisis have passed, it is often appropriate to invite parents to a public meeting to disseminate information on the school's postvention efforts and provide an overview of youth suicide. A consultant's participation in this meeting can help to reassure parents and legitimize the school's response. There is some question about the timing of such meetings. Confusion, anxiety, and the tendency to scapegoat are at their height within the first few days after a suicide. However, any perception that the school is avoiding parents will only build up tension. Whenever the meeting is held, its limits need to be recognized. Large meetings are not the place for exploring individual feelings and concerns. There can be provision for follow-up discussion groups led by crisis team members.

RESPONDING TO THE MEDIA

Publicity about the suicide should be minimized as much as possible, especially coverage that tends to sensationalize or glamorize the suicide. A school spokesperson should be appointed to insure accurate and consistent information. This spokesperson usually is the principal, the crisis team coordinator, or someone designated by the principal. In small school districts the superintendent may choose to act as spokesperson. The advantage of having a superintendent act as spokesperson is that the school is relieved of this task and can deal with the crisis. If there is a central coordinating committee, there should be close communication between the committee's spokesperson and the local school spokesperson. Involving the local newspaper editor, or designate, as a part of the community coordinating committee facilitates the cooperation of the press and other media. The school secretary or another designated person should have a fact sheet from which to respond to telephone inquiries when the spokesperson is unavailable. Never refuse a request for information. This only makes people angry and adds to the confusion. Reporters should not be given access to school grounds. Filming or interviewing students or staff on school grounds should be prohibited since the process of filming is likely to be intrusive.

The spokesperson needs to respond to the media in a timely and professional manner. However, the school should avoid becoming the principal source of information. Releasing details about the suicide is the responsibility of the medical examiner or other authorities. Never permit speculation as to why the student committed suicide. It is the family's sole prerogative to provide information about the victim. **The school can explain the positive steps of the postvention plan to help students through the crisis and provide information on where troubled youth can get help.** This is especially important in circumstances where the suicide becomes a major news story and the focus needs to be shifted from the school to the larger community.

LONG-TERM EFFECTS AND FOLLOW-UP

The aftermath of a suicide lasts a long time, While the most intense phase of the crisis—in the absence of any new incidents—will last only a few weeks, some effects may continue for a year or more. Individuals will differ considerably in the time it takes them to work through their feelings. Special counseling initiatives and outreach should continue as long as people need them. The school counselor, school psychologist or social worker, or community mental health professional may provide longer-term care instead of the crisis team. Certain situations such as sporting events, extracurricular activities, graduation, and the anniversary of the suicide itself, may reawaken the distress. The school should respond by being prepared with postvention measures as indicated.

Often after a school suicide, there is a call for staff training in prevention. Such training is not a substitute for postvention work and should not be instituted until well after the initial phase of the crisis.

The aftermath of a suicide can be one of the most stressful and painful experiences any school will have. It is also possible for the school to resolve the crisis in a manner that leaves it stronger, more resilient, and more caring. This does not mean that the feelings will ever go away completely. It does mean that individuals, organizations, and even whole communities can learn and grow from the experience.

ACTION STEPS IN BRIEF

Below is a review and summary of the major points of the postvention plan recommended by the American Association of Suicidology School Suicide Prevention Programs Committee:

1. Plan in advance of any crisis.
2. Select and train a crisis team.
3. Verify the report of a suicide from the medical examiner or police.
4. Schedule a meeting of the crisis team with the school principal.
5. Assess the situation and adjust the size of the team accordingly.
6. Disseminate information to faculty, students, and parents.
7. Follow the victim's classes throughout the day.
8. Arrange for counseling rooms.
9. Invite friends to join a support group or meet with team members individually.
10. Check records and provide counseling for all students identified as at risk.
11. Provide counseling or discussion opportunities for faculty.
12. Arrange for students and faculty to attend the funeral or memorial service.
13. Coordinate memorials.
14. Make a home visit.
15. Respond to media inquiries.
16. Link with the community as appropriate.
17. Follow up with continued counseling as needed.

Sample Faculty Memo

DATE:

TO: _____ Middle School Faculty and Staff

FROM: James Decker, Principal

RE: The Suicide of John Smith

We are asking you to discuss the death of John Smith, an eighth grade _____ Middle School student, with your class at the beginning of school. Some students will already be aware of his suicide from the 10:00 p.m. news on TV last night. Others will be learning of his death from you. It is recommended that you give your students an opportunity to hear the following facts from you, to ask questions, and to discuss their feelings. You can expect some students to be angry and upset as well as sad. Please be sensitive to their feelings.

John died last night at 8:00 p.m. He was found by his father and was rushed by an ambulance and paramedics to the emergency room of the county hospital where the trauma doctors and nurses were unable to revive him. He did not regain consciousness and died a half hour after he arrived. The medical examiner has ruled his death a suicide. His parents would like you to know that they have donated some of his organs so others may have a chance to live. We do not know why John choose to kill himself. Unfortunately, he did not realize what other options were available to help him with his problems. His solution was permanent and irreversible.

Students may be excused from classes for John's funeral if they bring written permission from a parent. Funeral arrangements are still pending. We will give you that information when we receive it. The family will be at the funeral home tomorrow evening if students wish to pay their respects and extend their sympathy. Some students may wish to make a donation to the Suicide and Crisis Center in John's memory. A box has been placed in the office to collect donations or any notes written to John's family.

The crisis team will be in the school building throughout today and the rest of the week. If you wish some assistance in discussing John's death with your class, a team member will come to your classroom. Please identify any student you think needs further help in dealing with this tragic event and send him or her to the counseling office.

Today may be a very difficult one for you as well as our students. A crisis team member will be in the teachers' lounge if you wish to talk further about the suicide.

Sample Letter to Parents

Dear Parents of _____ Middle School Students:

The _____ Middle School community was saddened to learn of the reported suicide of one of our students. The death of any young person is a loss that, in one way or another, diminishes each of us. The tragic circumstances of John Smith's death are perhaps more shocking and more difficult to accept.

We have asked the assistance of the crisis team to help our school community deal with this loss. We are doing everything we can to help your child and our faculty and staff through this tragic experience. You may anticipate more questions and a need to talk about the suicide at home.

John's funeral will be held at Grace Baptist Church, 428 Elm Street on Thursday at 10:30 a.m. Your child may be excused from school to attend the funeral with written permission from you. We encourage you to make arrangements to accompany him or her and you will need to provide your own transportation. The school will remain open for those students who choose not to attend the funeral.

John's classmates and teachers have decided to accept donations in his memory and will make a contribution to the Suicide and Crisis Center. Please contact the school office at ____-_____ for further information.

If you have any concerns regarding your child's reactions to this loss, Mrs. Jones, the school nurse, and Mr. Johnston, the school counselor, will be available to assist you.

Sincerely,

James Decker, Principal
_____ Middle School

CRISIS MANAGEMENT

- Remember the meaning of the term " crisis management."

- Be calm and supportive.

- Be nonjudgmental.

- Encourage self-disclosure.

- Acknowledge the reality of suicide as a choice, but do not "normalize" suicide as a choice.

- Listen actively and reinforce positively.

- Do not attempt in-depth counseling.

- Contact another professional.

- Ask questions to assess lethality.

CRISIS MANAGEMENT

MAKE CRISIS-MANAGEMENT DECISIONS

- Notify parents.

- Consider hospitalization.

- Write a contract.

- Organize a suicide watch.

STEPS IN POSTVENTION

- Plan in advance.

- Select and train a crisis team as part of the previous step.

- Verify report of suicide with medical examiner or police.

- Schedule crisis team meeting with school principal.

- Assess the situation and adjust team size accordingly.

- Disseminate information to faculty, students, and parents.

- Follow victim's classes throughout the day.

- Arrange for counseling rooms.

- Invite friends to be in a group or meet individually with a team member.

STEPS IN POSTVENTION

- Check records and provide counseling for all identified at-risk students.

- Provide counseling or discussion opportunities for faculty.

- Arrange for students and faculty to attend funeral.

- Coordinate memorials—use caution.

- Make home visit.

- Respond to media inquiries.

- Link with community as appropriate.

- Follow up with continued counseling as needed.

CHAPTER FIVE
INDIVIDUAL AND GROUP
COUNSELING OPTIONS

As noted in Chapter 2, schools are not ready to discuss suicide prevention with groups of students until options for individual and group counseling are in place. **(Even if administrative support, faculty/staff in-service, and preparation of crisis teams all have been accomplished, any effort at prevention, crisis management, or postvention will fail unless students can call on counseling and related services when seeking assistance for themselves or their friends.)**

Providing counseling options for students, particularly before an "attempt," is really the essence of suicide prevention. This may present a problem to those working in middle and secondary school settings if counselors are immersed in a variety of secondary responsibilities (hall monitoring, cafeteria duty, club sponsorship, etc.). By fifth or sixth grade students are faced with decisions about drugs, gang membership, expression of sexuality, coping with a dysfunctional family of origin, etc., this makes it imperative for schools and school districts to provide for the educational, career, and personal/social development of students differently from 10 or 20 years ago.

Although it is beyond the scope of this guide to provide a comprehensive plan for guidance and counseling in schools, an abbreviated version, adopted from the model developed by Gysbers and Henderson (1994) is presented for consideration and discussion. The plan that follows focuses on the three domains of educational, personal/social, and career development with services to students, faculty/staff, and parents delivered through four methods: the guidance curriculum, responsive services, individual planning, and system support. For a more comprehensive discussion, refer to the Gysbers and Henderson book.

DISTRICT PLAN: GUIDANCE AND COUNSELING
_____ SCHOOLS

Guidance and counseling in _____ Schools are an integral part of the district's educational program. As we move through the 1990s to the 21st century, it is imperative that faculty and staff at _____ Schools provide more emphasis and attention to the education of the whole person to enable students to become responsible, productive, and contributing members of society. Students of the 1990s are entitled to an education that assists them in the development of skills that will enable them to succeed in their choice of roles as family members, workers, friends, and participants in the community. Skills such as decision making, written and verbal communication, self-analysis, problem solving, information gathering and analysis, critical thinking, synthesis, assuming personal responsibility, dealing with feelings, analysis of one's behavior and its impact on others, and presentation of self in a confident, sensitive way are some of the life skills that productive, contributing members of a diverse society need to develop a strong self-identity.

Counselors and other student-service specialists believe they play vital and integral roles in the education of students because services offered to students, faculty, staff, and families are based on a number of premises, as listed below.

GUIDANCE AND COUNSELING IN _____ SCHOOLS:

1. Provide a vital link to the total instructional program of the school district.
2. Make available a "curriculum" based primarily on the needs of students.
3. Contain measurable student outcomes that address behaviors necessary for a person to function effectively.
4. Seek to help students attain educational excellence through individual excellence.
5. Are an integral part of the student's educational experience.
6. Encourage and include parent/teacher/community involvement.
7. Are designed to address the needs of all students at all educational levels, K–12.
8. Are consistent with expected developmental stages of personal/social development.
9. Provide developmental as well as preventive, crisis, remedial, and referral services.
10. Have identifiable outcomes for which guidance and counseling personnel have primary responsibility.
11. Are evaluated on stated goals and related student outcomes.

FOCUS OF SERVICES

Guidance and counseling in _____ Schools are focused on three major domains: *educational development, personal/social development,* and *career development.* Connected with each domain are several primary goals, each of which is linked with several desired student outcomes.

The Educational Development Domain

Goal. To facilitate the educational development of students by maintaining and enhancing their motivation to learn, striving to help them fulfill their potential, and helping them to accept responsibility for their own learning and to seek out new learning experiences.

Student outcomes.

- Increased development and use of study, reading, and mathematical skills.
- Use of available educational resources.

- Positive attitudes toward work and learning.

Examples of attainment.

- Demonstrated use of independent study skills.
- Thoughtful use of time as related to class time, personal/social, and career responsibilities and interests.
- Ability to use the resources available in the school and community.
- Ability to state the relationship between the curriculum and current and future career and life goals.
- Recognition of the need to stay "enrolled" as a lifelong learner.
- Capacity to develop, implement, and complete an individual educational plan.

The Personal/Social Development Domain

Goal one.   To facilitate the personal development of students by helping them learn to respect and understand themselves to improve their self-esteem and responsible behavior.

Student outcomes.

- Recognition of and respect for personal feelings, appearance, culture, and values.
- Enhanced self-esteem.
- Responsible behavior.

Examples of attainment.

- Awareness of strengths and weaknesses as part of a personal growth plan.
- Acceptance of physical appearance.
- Feeling and attitude changes based on a rational thinking process.
- Responsible decision making as part of a positive plan for personal well-being.
- Acceptance of responsibility for the outcome of past decision making.
- Assumption of personal responsibility for meeting needs while respecting the needs of others.
- Ability to state values on which decisions are based.
- Awareness of and respect for cultural differences between self and others.

Goal two.   To facilitate the social development of students by encouraging healthy interpersonal relationships and responsible behavior in school, the family, and the community.

Student outcomes.

- Effective interaction with individuals of all ages.
- Effective interaction with individuals from different ethnic cultural backgrounds.
- Enjoyment of interpersonal relationships.

Examples of attainment.

- Use of effective communication skills with diverse individuals and groups.
- Demonstration of helping, sharing, and cooperating.
- Sensitivity to social and human rights issues and interest in assuming responsibility for positive outcomes.
- Satisfying peer relationships.
- Ability to make informed and responsible decisions about sexual interactions and invitations to use alcohol and other substances.
- Willingness to access school and community support services if needed.
- Demonstrated knowledge of child development and realistic expectations for parenting (discipline for guidance instead of punishment).

The Career Development Domain

Goal.　　　To facilitate the career development of students by increasing their awareness of their career potential and helping them gain realistic perceptions of the relationships of their personal/social and educational goals to the world of work.

Student outcomes.

- Ability to relate personal feelings, attitudes, and values to the world of work.
- Insight into the relationship between current and future educational plans and the world of work.
- Awareness of the developmental nature of a "career" over a lifetime.

Examples of attainment.

- Recognition of the relationship between career goals and educational choices.
- Identification of life-style and its relationship to educational decisions and employment options.
- Ability to relate interests, values, and aptitudes to career choice.
- Awareness of the changing needs that affect career-related decisions throughout one's lifetime.

DELIVERY OF SERVICES

Educational, personal/social, and career development domains upon which guidance and counseling services are focused are delivered through four methods: *guidance curriculum, responsive services, individual planning,* and *system support.*

Guidance Curriculum

The guidance curriculum consists of structured/developmental experiences presented systematically and sequentially through classroom and group activities.

The object of the curriculum is for the students to attain specific outcomes. The guidance curriculum provides students with knowledge of growth and development, promotes their positive mental health, and assists in acquiring and using life skills. The curriculum is organized around three developmental domains: education, personal/social, and career.

While counselors' responsibilities include organization and implementation of the guidance curriculum, the cooperation and support of the entire student services team, faculty, and staff are necessary for its successful implementation. The guidance curriculum is delivered through such strategies as:

Classroom activities. Counselors team teach or assist in teaching guidance curriculum activities or units in classrooms. Guidance curriculum activities are not limited to one or two subjects. These activities may be conducted in the classroom, counseling office, or other school facilities.

Group activities. Counselors conduct groups outside the classroom to respond to students' identified interests or needs. Counselors plan and lead structured activities to increase the skills and knowledge of the students.

Parenting education. To be fully effective, materials presented through curricular offerings and supported in responsive services should be reinforced by the students' parents. An organized and structured approach to parenting education is an essential link to the successful attainment of student competencies.

Examples of guidance learning activities and themes within this component may include, but are not restricted, to the following:

- middle school advisory programs
- self-concept enhancement
- communication skills training
- peer relationship enhancement
- personal safety education
- substance-abuse programs
- post-high school decision-making information
- teaching study skills
- teaching decision-making skills
- career awareness programs
- career exploration activities
- preemployment skills development
- job preparation information

Responsive Services

Responsive services consist of activities designed to meet immediate needs and concerns of students. These needs or concerns require counseling, consultation, referral, or information. This component is available to all students and is often student-initiated. While counselors have special training and skills to respond to these needs and concerns, the cooperation and support of the entire student services team, faculty, and staff are necessary for successful implementation of this component. Responsive services are delivered through these strategies:

Consultation. Counselors and other student services team members consult with students, parents, teachers, other educators, and community agencies regarding strategies to help students.

Personal counseling. Counseling is provided in small groups or on an individual basis for students expressing difficulties with relationships, personal concerns, or normal developmental tasks. Personal counseling assists students in identifying problems, causes, alternatives, and possible consequences so that appropriate action can be taken.

Crisis counseling. Counseling and support are provided to students and their families facing emergency situations. Such counseling is normally short-term and temporary in nature. When necessary, appropriate referral sources are used.

Referral. Counselors use referral sources to enhance the school counseling program. These referral sources may include:

- mental health agencies
- employment and training programs
- vocational rehabilitation
- juvenile services
- social services

Individual Planning

Individual planning consists of activities that help students to plan, monitor, and manage their educational, personal/social, and career development. Individual planning generally is initiated in classroom and group activities, but it eventually becomes the focus of individual or group sessions with a counselor. Individual planning includes an annual review of each student's educational and career plans.

Individual appraisal. Counselors help students to assess and interpret their abilities, interests, skills, and achievements. Appropriate assessment information becomes an important component in developing immediate and long-range plans for students.

Individual advisement. Counselors help students in acquiring self-appraisal, personal/social, education, career, and labor market information. This information assists students to plan for and realize their personal, educational, and career aspirations.

Placement and follow-up. Counselors assist students in making transitions. They focus on giving information, advising, helping to establish linkages, counseling in the face of interpersonal conflict, and referral.

Examples of individual planning strategies include:

- career awareness
- role playing
- career exploration
- course selection
- career shadowing
- four-year plan development
- informational interviewing

- honors and awards programs
- business partnerships
- vocational education and training
- financial aid and scholarship information and application
- college and vocational school application

System Support

Program development and system support consist of management activities that establish, maintain, and enhance the total guidance and counseling program. Activities in this component provide support to the guidance and counseling system itself and to the school system as a whole. This component is implemented and carried out through activities in the following areas:

Professional development. Student services team members are involved regularly in updating their professional knowledge and skills. This may involve participation in regular school in-service training, attending meetings, completing postgraduate work, and contributing to the professional literature.

Staff/community public relations. Activities designed to orient the staff and community about student services through newsletters, local media, and school and community presentations. Serving on departmental curriculum committees and community or advisory boards are examples of involvement that generate community support.

Consultation with staff. Counselors and other student services team members consult with teachers and other staff members regularly to provide information and support to staff and to get feedback on emerging needs of students.

Research and development. Program evaluation, data analysis, follow-up studies, and the continued development and updating of services are some examples of the research and development work of counselors and other student services team members.

Community outreach. These activities are designed to help counselors become knowledgeable about community resources, employment opportunities, and local labor market information. Outreach may involve counselors visiting local businesses, industries, and social service agencies on a periodic basis.

In-service. Counselors and other student services team members can provide in-service instruction to staff members in areas covered by the curriculum and areas of special concern such as youth suicide, at-risk students, or parenting education.

Curriculum development support. This is focused on review and revision of guidance curriculum materials. Middle school advisory curricula provide an example of guidance curriculum.

REFERRAL SERVICES: GUIDANCE AND COUNSELING _____ SCHOOLS

If the school district or school cannot make a commitment to providing counseling, then arrangements must be made for referral to community agencies and private practitioners. It is important to provide adolescents and their families with a variety of referral possibilities along with information on fee schedules. There may be some question about whether the school district will be liable for the cost of such counseling if the referral is made by the school. (This issue should be explored by legal counsel retained by the district.) The dilemma, of course, is that unless counseling takes place when a suicidal adolescent has been identified, an attempt or a completion probably will take place. If the school is aware of a teenager's suicidal preoccupation and does not act in the best interests of that teenager, families may bring suit against the district. (This issue will be discussed further in Chapter 8.)

Every guidance and counseling department should have developed a compendium of referral possibilities for students and their families. This compendium should include options for *developmental counseling* as well as crisis counseling. If your school or district has developed such a list of referral possibilities, you may wish to insert it behind this page.

DISTRICT PLAN
GUIDANCE AND COUNSELING

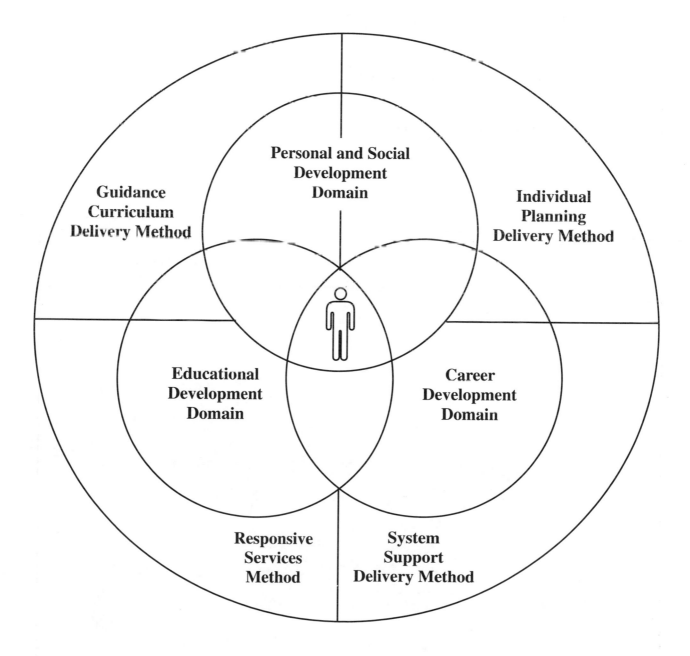

DISTRICT PLAN
GUIDANCE AND COUNSELING

Focused on three major domains:

- **Educational Development**

- **Personal/Social Development**

- **Career Development**

DISTRICT PLAN
GUIDANCE AND COUNSELING

THE EDUCATIONAL DEVELOPMENT DOMAIN

Goal: **To facilitate the educational development of students by maintaining and enhancing their motivation to learn, striving to help them fulfill their potential, and helping them to accept responsibility for their own learning and to seek out new learning experiences.**

DISTRICT PLAN
GUIDANCE AND COUNSELING

THE PERSONAL/SOCIAL DEVELOPMENT DOMAIN

Goal: **To facilitate the personal development of students by helping them learn to respect and understand themselves to improve their self-esteem and responsible behavior.**

Goal: **To facilitate the personal development of students by encouraging healthy interpersonal relationships and responsible behavior in school, the family, and the community.**

DISTRICT PLAN
GUIDANCE AND COUNSELING

THE CAREER DEVELOPMENT DOMAIN

Goal: To facilitate the career development of students by increasing their awareness of their career potential and helping them gain perceptions of the relationships of their personal/social and educational goals to the world of work.

DISTRICT PLAN
GUIDANCE AND COUNSELING

DELIVERY OF SERVICES

Educational, personal/social, and career development domains upon which guidance and counseling services are focused are delivered through four methods:

- Guidance curriculum

- Responsive services

- Individual planning

- System support

DISTRICT PLAN
GUIDANCE AND COUNSELING

GUIDANCE CURRICULUM

- The guidance curriculum consists of structured/developmental experiences presented systematically and sequentially through classroom and group activities.

- The guidance curriculum provides students with knowledge of growth and development, promotes their positive mental health, and assists in acquiring and using life skills.

DISTRICT PLAN
GUIDANCE AND COUNSELING

RESPONSIVE SERVICES

- **Responsive services consist of activities designed to meet immediate needs and concerns of students. This component is available to all students and is often student-initiated.**

- **Responsive services are delivered through these strategies:**

    Consultation

    Personal counseling

    Crisis counseling

    Referral

DISTRICT PLAN
GUIDANCE AND COUNSELING

INDIVIDUAL PLANNING

- **Individual planning consists of activities that help students to plan, monitor, and manage their educational, personal/social, and career development.**

- **Individual planning generally is initiated in classroom and group activities, but it eventually becomes the focus of individual or group sessions with a counselor. It includes:**

    Appraisal

    Advisement

    Placement and follow-up

DISTRICT PLAN
GUIDANCE AND COUNSELING

SYSTEM SUPPORT

- Program development and system support consist of management activities that establish, maintain, and enhance the total guidance and counseling program.

- This component is implemented through activities in the following areas:

  Professional development

  Staff/community public relations

  Consultation with staff

  Research and development

  Community outreach

  In-service

  Curriculum development support

CHAPTER SIX
PARENT EDUCATION

If the school district or school is unable to provide counseling, then arrangements for referral to community agencies and private practitioners must be made. It is important to provide adolescents and their families with a variety of referral possibilities along with information on fee schedules. There may be some question about whether the school district is liable for the cost of such counseling if the referral is made by the school. (This issue should be explored by the district's legal counsel.) The dilemma, of course, is that unless counseling takes place as soon as possible after a suicidal adolescent has been identified, it is quite probable that he or she will attempt suicide. If the school is aware of a teenager's suicidal preoccupation and does not act in the best interests of such a teenager, families may bring suit against the district. (This issue will be discussed further in Chapter 8.)

One of the first things you may wish to do with a parent group is use some of the material in Chapter 3. Most parents find the information about myths and the suicidal profile quite helpful. The same overheads also can be used. Parents usually have a number of questions about this information; be sure to allow time for discussion.

After the above material has been presented and discussed, you may wish to add portions of the following information, depending upon the amount of time available (McCoy, 1982; Rodesh, undated). Please be sure to save time to describe what your building or district is doing to prevent suicide attempts and/or manage crises.

WHAT CAN PARENTS DO IF THEY THINK THERE IS A PROBLEM?

Here are some suggestions to help answer this question:

1. **Trust your feelings**. Many times your instincts are correct. You may notice changes in your child that tell you something is wrong.

2. **Be aware of signs**. If there is a past suicide attempt; if your son or daughter has intentionally hurt him/herself; if it appears that your son or daughter is frequently involved in careless or life-threatening behaviors, or involved in

numerous accidents; if your son or daughter has said something that sounds like he or she would like to die, such as, "Things would be better if I weren't around," or "If one more thing goes wrong I'll blow my brains out"—all could be indicators of suicidal intent.

Do not be afraid to:

Ask: Do not be afraid to ask your son or daughter if he or she is thinking of suicide or death. You may think mentioning the subject will suggest the idea, but if your child is as upset as it seems, he/she already has the idea. It is better to talk about it out in the open. Let your child know some of the changes you have noticed in his/her behavior that have caused you concern. Let your child know if you are afraid. More than likely, if your child is seriously considering suicide, he/she is afraid too. If your child indicates that he or she has considered suicide, ask whether your child has a plan as to how and/or when. Your discussion will not prompt your child to go ahead with the plan, but will let your child know that you can help. However, remove all accessible methods (e.g., guns, medications, etc.) from your home.

Listen: Do not be judgmental of your child, the thought of suicide, or the situation that seems to be causing it. Do not point out how much better off he or she is than other teens; this will only make your child feel more guilty and worthless. Do focus on feelings and reflect both the message and the feelings back. Do let your child know you care. When someone talks about suicide, we all have three options in how to respond: we can *negate, ignore,* or *affirm.*

If we *negate* ("You really can't mean that"), your child feels as though no one understands the extent of his or her pain.

If we *ignore* ("Let's go for a ride"), your child cannot be sure if you heard what was said.

But if we *affirm* ("You must be in a lot of pain"), it lets your child know that you have some idea of how desperate things are. It reinforces that you understand and that you care.

Get Help: Believe what your child is saying. Letting your child know you believe him or her and want to help is important.

WHERE TO GET HELP

From Family and Friends

Although friends and family can be useful in helping a suicidal person, sometimes their intervention will not help. Sometimes friends and family may be involved intimately in the disturbance that is leading toward suicide. In such cases, a person outside the family may be the only one who can work productively with the suicidal adolescent. A suicidal adolescent may be seriously disturbed and beyond the skills of a nonprofessional. In this case there are a number of resources to which an adolescent at risk and those concerned about him or her can turn. Mental health professionals can assess the seriousness of the suicidal risk and recommend a course of action. Treatment options include individual outpatient counseling/therapy, family counseling/therapy, group counseling/therapy, or short-term hospitalization. The counseling/therapy may be short-term, crisis-oriented, or may continue over a long period of time.

From Professionals

Professional help, which means anything from psychoanalysis to family therapy to crisis counseling, is found in a variety of settings and with a number of different mental health professionals. Some people may use counseling/therapy to improve their communication skills and prevent major problems; many more seek help when a crisis occurs and they are unable to help themselves or their children. Whether professional help is used as a preventive measure or in a crisis situation, counseling/therapy can help in a number of ways:

1. **Counseling/therapy can help you understand and come to terms with your own past**. With the help of a professional, you can discover and accept what has occurred in the past, learn new ways of seeing yourself and your alternatives, and develop new skills for loving yourself and others.

2. **Counseling/therapy can help you and your family get feelings out into the open, in a nonthreatening way**, with a skilled professional who can moderate the discussion and help you deal with your feelings in a constructive way.

3. **Counseling/therapy helps you improve your communication skills**, express feelings clearly, and listen with new understanding to those you love.

4. **Counseling/therapy can help an adolescent find his or her own feelings**, begin to build a more positive self-image, and make changes that will bring more hope into the adolescent's life, easing the depression.

5. **Counseling/therapy can help families change patterns of interaction that create problems**. It helps block patterns of communication that cause misunderstandings.

6. **Counseling/therapy can give you hope in the midst of crisis**. Professional help is not a panacea. The possibilities mentioned above are ideal results; they are not inevitable. How valuable counseling/therapy will be for you and your family will depend on a number of factors, including how soon you seek help, how carefully this help is chosen, your attitude about it, how you use the help (how hard you are willing to work, to compromise, and to risk change), and how willing other family members are to do the same.

What Kind of Help Is Available?

Many different approaches or types of counseling/therapy are provided by mental health professionals.

1. **Individual counseling/therapy** involves intensive work with current problems, past experiences, self-concept, and other matters of importance to the person in treatment. The counselor/therapist may be a psychiatrist, psychologist, marriage counselor, family counselor or child counselor/ therapist, psychiatric social worker, or psychiatric nurse.

2. **Family counseling/therapy** treats the family as a unit, focusing on the concept that most problems exist within a family system, not totally within an individual family member.

3. In **group counseling/therapy**, a mental health professional presides over a group of usually unrelated individuals who share feelings, experiences, and observations in an effort to identify and resolve problems and conflict.

4. Another source of help is **self-help groups**, sometimes called support groups. In these groups, members share common concerns and are offered something very important in their recovery: the understanding and help of others who have gone

through similar experiences. Self-help groups are not meant to replace counseling/therapy, but they are an alternative to coping alone. Support groups have been established for a number of reasons, including support for survivors of suicide, suicide attempters, and parents of acting-out adolescents.

Who Are the Counselors and Therapists?

1. **A psychiatrist** is a medical doctor (MD) who has special training beyond medical school in treating mental and emotional illnesses. Only a psychiatrist or other physician can prescribe drugs, which may be needed to treat severe depression and other mental disorders.

   Clients going to a community mental health clinic (CMHC) may get a prescription from the clinic's medical director or from a psychiatrist who works as a consultant to mental health professionals.

2. **A licensed psychologist** who is an evaluator and therapist is usually a clinical, counseling, or school psychologist who has a Ph.D., Ed.D., or Psy.D. degree plus several years of supervised clinical experience, and has passed a licensing exam. Under some special circumstances, a psychologist may also be trained at the master's level in psychology.

3. **A licensed professional counselor or therapist** has a master's or doctoral degree in marriage/family, child counseling, counseling, or psychology. These counselors can focus on the family as a unit and on helping to improve communication. Such counselors are licensed by the state board that licenses professional counselors and therapists.

4. **A clinical social worker** is trained to help individuals and families deal with a range of economic, social, and personal problems. Training includes individual and group marital and family therapy, psychosocial diagnosis, and community organization. A licensed social worker has completed a bachelor's, master's, or doctoral degree in social work or a related field.

5. **A psychiatric nurse clinician** is a registered nurse who has at least a master's degree in mental health nursing and supervised experience in working with emotionally distressed individuals.

6. **Helpers at crisis centers and hot lines** may be volunteers with several weeks or months of training in crisis intervention—i.e., listening skills, problem solving, and referring to appropriate community resources. Many crisis centers and hot lines have licensed mental health supervisors present who work in conjunction with the volunteers.

How Do You Find a Person Qualified to Treat Suicidal Adolescents?

Craig Rupp, a parent and cofounder of SPARE, a suicide prevention foundation in Denver, Colorado, has identified some areas to consider when looking for a therapist to treat suicidal adolescents and their families.

1. **Review the counselor's or therapist's qualifications**. Is this professional trained in crisis intervention and experienced in dealing with suicidal adolescents?

2. **Ask about the counselor's or therapist's "track" record in treating adolescents and their families**. How many drop out of treatment, how many make future attempts, and how many complete suicide?

3. **Ask how available the counselor/therapist is** to the adolescent and to the family during times of crisis.

4. **Evaluate whether the counselor/therapist likes working with adolescents** and can develop a relationship with the adolescent.

Rupp advocates thorough questioning of the person selected to provide treatment to the adolescent and the family. The adolescent and the family must be able to develop a relationship with the therapist to have their needs met.

What Settings Are Available?

Help is available in a variety of settings. You may go to a counselor/therapist in private practice, to a private clinic, or to a community mental health center (CMHC). If your adolescent is experiencing considerable distress, or is in imminent danger of suicide, or if your family is in too much turmoil to solve existing problems, care can be provided at a hospital, residential treatment center, group home, or foster home.

The settings you select will depend on a number of factors, including your financial resources (private therapists and clinics may be more expensive than community mental health clinics), how immediate the crisis is (you may sometimes encounter a waiting period for appointments in any setting), and what type of counseling/therapy the family prefers.

Cost is a major consideration. Some counselors/therapists in private practice charge a flat fee, while others work on a sliding-fee scale. Flat or sliding-fee scales also may be available at private clinics. All community mental health centers (CMHC) operate on a sliding-fee scale.

Insurance coverage for counseling/therapy varies a great deal; psychiatric illnesses often do not have the same coverage as physical illnesses. Sometimes coverage is limited to services provided by certain mental health professionals. Check with your insurance company to see what is covered before you choose a mental health professional.

PARENT EDUCATION

WHAT CAN PARENTS DO?

- **Trust your feelings.**

- **Be aware of signs.**

DO NOT BE AFRAID TO:

- **Ask.**

- **Listen.**

- **Get help.**

PARENT EDUCATION

WHAT KIND OF HELP IS AVAILABLE?

- **Individual counseling/therapy**

- **Family counseling/therapy**

- **Group counseling/therapy**

- **Self-help groups**

- **Short-term hospitalization**

PARENT EDUCATION

WHO ARE THE COUNSELORS AND THERAPISTS?

- **Psychiatrist**

- **Licensed psychologist**

- **Licensed professional counselor**

- **Clinical social worker**

- **Psychiatric nurse clinician**

- **A crisis center-trained volunteer (listening and referral only)**

CHAPTER SEVEN
CLASSROOM PRESENTATIONS

Debate about the safety of adolescent suicide-prevention programs that contain an educational component for to adolescents continues. This debate is similar to the one that emerged years ago when schools initiated staff development and classroom presentations on physical and sexual abuse. A number of experts advocate education and discussion efforts that are focused on students in conjunction with a school-wide suicide prevention effort (Capuzzi, 1986; Capuzzi & Golden, 1988; Curran, 1987; Ross, 1980; Sudak, Ford, & Rushforth, 1984). **The key point to remember is that no discussion of suicide should be initiated with students until all adults in the "system" (school district) have been prepared properly.**

Providing adolescents with an appropriate forum by which they can receive accurate information, ask questions, and learn about how to get help for themselves and their friends does not precipitate suicidal preoccupation or attempts (Capuzzi, 1988). Since newspaper and television reports of individual and cluster suicides usually do not include adequate education on the topic, and since many films have presented the act of suicide unrealistically or have romanticized it, it is important for schools to address the problem in a way that is informative and encourages young people to reach out for help before they reach the point of despair.

A carefully prepared and well-presented classroom presentation made by a member of the school's core team (or another presenter who has expertise on the topic) is essential. Such a presentation should include information on causes, myths, and symptoms as well as how to obtain help through the school. *Under no circumstances should media be used in which adolescents are shown a suicide plan.*

At the elementary level, school faculty should not present suicide prevention programs; their efforts are better focused on developmental counseling and classroom presentations directed at helping children overcome traits (such as low self-esteem or poor communication skills) that may put them at risk for suicidal behavior later. Although these efforts should be continued through the secondary level, middle and high school students are better served through presentations that address adolescent suicide directly. (Middle and high school students almost always have direct or indirect experience with suicide and appreciate the opportunity to learn and ask questions.)

TEACHING ABOUT ADOLESCENT SUICIDE:
FOR MIDDLE AND HIGH SCHOOL CORE OR CRISIS TEAMS

Teaching about suicide is not an easy task; death is an emotional subject. Most of us have unresolved issues around death and suicide that complicate teaching this subject. You may find yourself working through some of your own issues at the same time that you are helping your students.

Rationale

There are a number of reasons to address suicide with middle and high school students:

1. To provide students with a clear, realistic image of what suicide is about, including the consequences for victims and their families and friends.

2. To provide students with the knowledge to recognize dangerous patterns in themselves or their peers.

3. To familiarize students with school and community resources for accessing help for themselves or their peers.

4. To bring suicide out in the open by legitimizing it as a topic of discussion.

5. To reduce myths and ideation about suicide through clear and honest discussion.

Preparation

Some staff members may think that discussing suicide may give students the idea or encourage attempts. Actually, opening up lines of communication helps students come forward. Students need to hear about depression and its link to alcohol and drug use in numerous adolescent suicides. When we don't discuss these topics, we isolate further the students who need help the most. In fact, not discussing these dangers is the very worst thing we can do. It is true that discussions can sometimes lead at-risk students to come forward. This allows knowledgeable staff to be supportive and refer the student to professional help.

You should send a letter home to alert parents of the suicide discussions. It is hoped that parents already will have taken advantage of the parent education opportunity you have provided.

Teaching about suicide is different from teaching about other areas of the curriculum such as math or English. The unit should not be graded. An atmosphere of trust in the classroom is essential. No student should be asked to share anything he or she does not wish to share; privacy must be respected.

Crisis team members are people too. It is a positive experience for students to see them participate in the discussion as well. Their role is not one of a counselor/therapist; they are there to share, listen, and be supportive. During this short unit, it is wise to be available to students outside the classroom; students may want to share experiences or ask questions privately.

Lesson Plans

The three lesson plans in this chapter form the basis for classroom discussion. These discussions should be conducted by crisis team members who have practiced presenting the information. Such discussions should never be conducted in large auditoriums or assemblies.

It may be possible to present the information in conjunction with a school's drug and alcohol program since so many suicidal adolescents also have substance abuse problems. Other than the overheads recommended for use in the three following lessons plans, no other films or videos have been suggested. Many such films and videos are poorly done or actually show a suicide being committed. Your school or district crisis team can develop additional lesson plans if it is possible to meet with student groups for longer periods of time.

LESSON ONE
ACQUIRING KNOWLEDGE ABOUT
SUICIDAL MYTHS

Myths and fallacies concerning suicide abound. Knowledge must replace ignorance if students are to help themselves and others.

Objective

To inform students of the myths and fallacies surrounding suicide and to replace them with facts.

Time Requirement

One class period.

Materials

1. "Test Your Own Knowledge" questionnaire.
2. "Understanding the Myths" overheads from Chapter 3.
3. "Frequently Asked Questions About Suicide" handout.

Instructions to the Crisis Team Member

1. The presenter should provide a copy of the "Test Your Own Knowledge" questionnaire to each student.
2. Explain that this is not a test. The papers will not be graded, nor will the presenter collect the papers.
3. Ask students to circle T for true, for F for false.
4. After students have finished marking their responses, the presenter should provide the correct answers.
5. As each correct response is read, the presenter should encourage discussion of the statement. Use the "Understanding the Myths" overheads during this process.
6. After discussing the true/false questionnaire, divide students into groups of four and give the students copies of Handout #1: "Frequently Asked Questions About Suicide" and have them read through it and discuss the information in their small groups. Provide opportunity for total group discussion as time permits.

Test Your Own Knowledge

1.   T   F   Adolescents who talk about suicide never attempt suicide.

2.   T   F   Suicide usually happens without warning.

3.   T   F   Adolescents from rich families attempt suicide more often than adolescents from poor families.

4.   T   F   Once an adolescent is suicidal, he or she is suicidal forever.

5.   T   F   If an adolescent attempts suicide and survives, he or she will never try it again.

6.   T   F   Adolescents who complete or attempt suicide always leave notes.

7.   T   F   Most adolescent suicides happen late at night or in the predawn hours.

8.   T   F   Never use the word suicide when talking to adolescents because using the word gives some adolescents the idea.

9.   T   F   Every adolescent who attempts suicide is depressed.

10.   T   F   Suicide is hereditary.

Handout #1

Frequently Asked Questions About Suicide

1. ***Why do people commit suicide?*** People who commit suicide have intense feelings of helplessness and hopelessness and don't see any other way out. Revenge also may be a motive.

2. ***What do teenagers commit suicide?*** Teenagers who commit suicide are feeling unloved/ rejected or perceive themselves as failures in their families or in relationships.

3. ***Is it true that people attempt suicide as a cry for help?*** The suicide attempt is often a conscious or unconscious way to get others to recognize just how badly the individual is feeling.

4. ***If someone in the family has committed suicide, are others in the family tempted to commit suicide when they have problems?*** If someone in the family has committed suicide, other family members may be more tempted because that behavior has been modeled for them.

5. ***Do people ever attempt suicide to get attention or to get others to feel sorry for them?*** Anyone who attempts suicide to get attention desperately needs attention. It is tragic when young people feel they need to bargain with their lives to have their problems taken seriously.

6. ***If a person attempts suicide and fails, what is the likelihood of trying again?*** Ten percent of those who complete suicide have made a prior suicide attempt; however, many people who receive appropriate help after a suicide attempt may never become suicidal again.

7. ***Is it true that people who attempt to kill themselves really don't want to die?*** Most people who kill themselves are ambivalent about whether to live or die right up to the moment of death. They want to live *and* die at the same time.

8. ***Will a person who is deeply depressed always become suicidal?*** While it is true that suicidal feelings often develop in a person who is deeply depressed, the fact that one is depressed does not mean that person will become suicidal.

9. ***Does anyone ever attempt suicide impulsively and then become sorry for making such an attempt?*** At a particular moment a person may find the emotional pain experienced absolutely intolerable. In that short period a suicide attempt made impulsively might be regretted later.

10. ***Does taking drugs or alcohol increase one's chances of becoming suicidal?*** Taking drugs and alcohol can exaggerate painful feelings to a point where the feelings are intolerable. In that state, a person who otherwise would not go that far might attempt suicide.

11. ***How can one help a person who is suicidal?*** A person who is feeling that life is too painful is usually feeling very worthless and unloved. Showing such an individual some real caring by listening and accepting feelings, staying close, and getting others to be supportive can help an individual immeasurably to feel life that may be worth living.

12. ***How does talking about suicide help prevent it?*** Talking about suicide diffuses some of the intensity of these feelings. It helps to connect the person to the help that is needed. It creates a climate of caring and helps to break through the loneliness the person is experiencing.

13. ***Is suicide or attempted suicide against the law?*** Suicide or attempted suicide used to be against the law. In some states, it is only within the last decade that suicide has ceased to be a crime. It is still illegal to assist someone in committing suicide (e.g., euthanasia).

14. ***Is a person who attempts suicide mentally ill?*** The majority of people who attempt suicide are not mentally ill but are feeling that their lives are intolerable. Because of a kind of tunnel vision, they are unable to see any other way out except suicide.

15. ***What effects does a suicide have on the individual's remaining family and relatives?*** The survivors of a suicide are left to struggle with complex feelings of rage, guilt, despair, grief, shame, etc. Recovery from the loss of a loved one by suicide is the hardest form of grief to resolve.

16. ***Why do some people keep a suicide in the family secret?*** Some people keep this secret out of fear of being blamed and socially ostracized. While this has been true in the past, much of the stigma is lifting and people are dealing with suicide more directly and honestly. Many support groups, such as The Samaritans, help suicidal individuals cope with their feelings of loneliness, depression, and emotional pain.

17. ***What are the most common methods used by teenagers to commit suicide?*** Lethal methods used by teenagers for attempting suicide are hanging, guns, carbon monoxide poisoning, jumping, and drug overdoses. Car accidents account for many deaths, but it is often difficult to determine whether the death is suicide or an accident.

18. ***Is there a particular hour of the day that is the most common time for attempting suicide?*** Young people, who are probably the most ambivalent suicides, tend to make attempts in the morning or around dinnertime, when the likelihood of rescue is possible.

19. ***Is there any particular group or class of people who are more likely to become suicidal?*** Suicide takes place in all levels of society. Teenagers who have experienced recent losses; who are Native American; who have a gay, lesbian, or bisexual orientation; who are chronically or terminally ill; or who have made a prior attempt (without receiving follow-up counseling) may be in a higher risk category.

20. ***How many teenagers each year actually succeed in killing themselves? How many more make attempts on their own lives?*** According to current statistics, more than 2,000 teenagers between the ages of 10 and 19 succeed in killing themselves each year. For older teens, 12% of all deaths are the result of suicide. As many as 300,000 teenagers attempt to kill themselves each year. Since many possible suicides and attempted suicides are listed as accidents, the numbers are probably much higher.

21. ***Do more men or women make attempts on their lives?*** Although many more women than men make attempts on their lives, more men actually succeed in killing themselves. This is because men who try usually use more lethal methods such as guns. Women are more likely to use pills.

22. ***Does everyone think about committing suicide at least once in his or her lifetime?*** Most people will have fleeting thoughts of suicide at some point in their lives.

—Anonymous

LESSON TWO
DEVELOPING AN AWARENESS OF THE SIGNS SIGNALING SUICIDE

Being able to recognize the warning signs when someone is suicidal is essential in preventing suicide. These signs are common and are apparent in about 80% of those who attempt or who succeed in killing themselves. When several warning signs are present, active intervention and help is called for. The best way to know whether someone is suicidal is to ask what that person means by a particular statement or action. A straightforward question ("Do you want to kill yourself?") is imperative.

Objectives

1. To inform students of the typical signs indicating impending suicide.
2. To help students interpret these warning signs.
3. To convince students to react to these signs by seeking help from a significant adult to save a life.

Time Requirement

One class period (minimum).

Materials

1. "Recognizing the Profile" overheads from Chapter 3.

Instructions to the Crisis Team Member

1. Use the "Recognizing the Profile" overheads to present information about the suicidal adolescent. Take time to engage students in as much discussion as possible.
2. Divide students into groups of four and have them formulate questions they still have about adolescent suicide. Have a spokesperson from each group raise questions and engage the class in follow-up discussion.

LESSON THREE
HOW TO HELP A FRIEND

Perhaps the most serious crisis facing us today is isolation. Invisible walls isolate instead of protect. Our primitive ancestors cowered fearfully in their various forms of shelter; modern man just cowers. We call ours the great age of communication with myriad devices to speed our messages along. We spend millions of dollars to make contact with intelligent life forms in outer space. Down here, we are so busy talking *at* each other that we don't know what it is to talk *with* each other or to listen, really listen, to each other.

Objectives
1. To help students learn to listen.
2. To help students encourage friends to get help.

Time Requirement
One class period (minimum).

Materials
1. Role-play situations.

Instructions for Role Playing
Some useful techniques to help someone at risk of attempting or committing suicide are:

*   Ask if the person is thinking about suicide.
*   Listen without being critical.
*   Be honest—you cannot keep the person's suicide plans a secret.
*   Be empathetic.
*   Get help from a faculty or staff member in your school.

After discussing each of the above, ask for two volunteers to role play one of the attached situations, emphasizing the above techniques. Be sure students know how to get help in their school for a friend about whom they are concerned.

Role-play Situations
1. Randy: "Hey Kathy! Wait up. I haven't seen you for at least a couple of weeks. Have you been sick?"

    Kathy: "No, but I wish I was."

    Randy: "What does that mean?"

    Kathy: "Oh nothing, never mind."

    Randy: "You know, you've been different since your mom got sick. Is everything OK?"

Kathy: "Not really..."

2. Zach: "That was really a weird poem you wrote in class. You really wouldn't want to be dead would you?"

    Tom: "Sometimes I don't think I deserve to be alive."

    Zach: "What do you mean?"

    Tom: "Well, like my brother who died in Desert Storm. He was better than me. I'd like to die and have him come back . . ."

3. Bill: "Hey, Jack, did you see Susan at lunch? She was with that new kid. I thought you were going out with her."

    Stan: "I saw her, alright. She didn't want to go out with someone like me anymore anyway. She's gonna be sorry tomorrow. Just watch."

CHAPTER EIGHT
LEGAL ASPECTS OF ADOLESCENT SUICIDE PREVENTION

The legal issues surrounding adolescent suicide and schools are exceedingly complex, and many of the ones presented here have not been clearly decided. Your school *must seek legal* counsel when one of the issues discussed in this section arises. The law differs by state and, occasionally, by community; therefore, only an attorney familiar with the law in your area can provide your school or school district with accurate advice. I hope to provide sufficient information about school policy, documentation, negligence, privacy and confidentiality issues, and suicide laws throughout the United States to illustrate when it is necessary to contact legal counsel.

SCHOOL POLICY

The best insurance against legal difficulties is written school policy that is known and followed by all school personnel. This means that the school should adopt policies covering all of the issues surrounding student suicide, including confidentiality, suicide attempts, and postvention. This policy should be written in conjunction with the school attorney or at least reviewed by the attorney. Although it may take time, energy, and money, it will help prevent lawsuits. In addition, during the stress connected with a suicidal crisis, faculty and staff will appreciate having clear guidelines to follow. Not having to worry about the legal correctness of their actions will enable faculty and staff to concentrate their energy on the truly important issues surrounding suicide.

Once policies have been written and are in place, the job is not finished; they need to be disseminated. Every school or school district employee who works with students should be aware of and familiar with the school's policy on suicide. In addition, they should be instructed to follow it when necessary.

DOCUMENTATION

Thorough documentation and record keeping are essential to maintain legal viability. In his review of 32 suicide or attempted suicide cases, Irwin N. Perr, a medical doctor and attorney, found that cases in which the defendant was found liable were due mainly to a lack of documentation of the actions that were taken. Perr (1985) states, "one who proclaims conformity to good practices can verify that practice by documentation; if the documentation is lacking, then that party is crippled in demonstrating what he has done" (p. 214).

Proper documentation enables the school to recreate what actually occurred. Records must be made immediately for two reasons. First, records are more likely to be accurate when the events are fresh. Second, if a lawsuit is filed later, "contemporaneous notes enhance the writer's credibility" (Perr, 1985, p. 215), and credibility is an important factor in the outcome of any lawsuit.

Proper documentation procedures should be spelled out in the school's policy. Perhaps a form including the questions discussed in the Crisis Management section of Chapter 4 could be made available to all members of the crisis team to help document suicide threats. Whatever the form, school policy must state that documentation is required, it should provide the form these records should take, and it should specify when the records should be made.

It is vital that all documentation be kept confidential and be shared with other staff members strictly on a need-to-know basis. This issue will be discussed more thoroughly later.

NEGLIGENCE

Although a complete discussion of negligence as it relates to adolescent suicide and schools is well beyond the scope of this book, this chapter will provide sufficient information to enable school faculty and staff to know when it is appropriate to contact the school attorney.

To sustain a cause of action for negligence, the injured student/person (plaintiff) must fulfill four requirements. The school (defendant) must have had a **duty** to protect or take care of the student; the school must have failed (or **breached the duty**) to protect or take care of the student; this failure must have **caused** the student's injury (or suicide/suicide attempt); and the **injury** must be compensable to the person bringing suit. These four elements will be discussed with regard to possible issues for a school when a student threatens, attempts suicide, or completes suicide. The issues that have been discussed by the courts and legal scholars are by no means exhaustive and, if you experience a case that raises questions, your best strategy is to consult an attorney.

Duty

Generally, duty requires that when people act they do so with reasonable care not to injure others. This issue could come up when providing suicide prevention education, counseling a potentially suicidal student, or disseminating information during postvention after a suicide or attempted suicide. Again, it should be stressed that appropriate school policy should be established and in place to cover the above situations.

When acting, this duty is fairly straightforward; an individual needs to act reasonably to protect others against foreseeable risk of harm. If the school is providing information or counseling, it should do so in a reasonable manner to decrease, rather than increase, the likelihood that a suicide or suicide attempt will occur.

The courts have consistently held, in cases unrelated to student suicides, that because "a child lacks a degree of discretion and maturity...the duty owed him is greater than that owed to an adult (*Ballard v. Polly*, 1975, p. 898). Thus, "a school owes it to its charges to exercise such care of them as a parent of ordinary prudence would observe in comparable circumstances" (*Ballard v. Polly*, 1975, p. 899–900). However, the court in this case also made clear that it did not intend to imply "that a school is an absolute insurer of the safety of its pupils" (*Ballard v. Polly*, 1975, p. 899). Courts have not yet determined whether schools will be held to a higher standard of care in suicide-related cases.

According to Drukteinis (1985), "there is...an increasing trend to regard the victim's acts as involuntary and to find someone else responsible...for...failing to prevent" (p. 77) the suicide.

In suicide-related negligence cases, the duty argued is usually an omission, or failure to act, rather than a duty when acting to act reasonably. As a general rule, courts are reluctant to impose an affirmative duty (a requirement to take action) on defendants. The court will look for a special relationship between the defendant and the plaintiff that required the defendant to act. The court would have to find that the school "was in a position to know about the suicide potential (i.e., it was foreseeable) and that [the school] failed to take measures to prevent the suicide from occurring" (Drukteinis, 1985, p. 73). Knuth (1979) states in her discussion of special relationships that such a relationship exists when "one of the parties places himself in a superior position as caretaker of the other, who depends upon that caretaker either entirely or with respect to a particular matter" (p. 990).

According to Schwartz (1971):

> Although schools have an affirmative duty to exercise reasonable supervisory control over their students to prevent accidents, it is clear that the amount of knowledge and control a non-boarding school usually has over a student would be insufficient to charge school personnel or the school itself with the duty of protecting a potentially suicidal student. (p. 253)

However, three cases stand out as possible harbingers of potential liability for schools. In *McBride v. State* (1968), the court applied this special duty to a boarding school run by the state. However, the facts in this case were unique. First, this was a boarding facility, where the student was under the supervision of surrogate parents. Second, he was physically punished (which was strictly against the rules), then left alone, where he hanged himself.

In a public nonboarding school setting only one case has established the potential for liability for omission or failure to act. In *Kelson v. City of Springfield* (1985), a student shot himself after brandishing a gun in class and then being confronted by a police officer. The court ruled that there was potential liability for schools under "a duty to provide suicide prevention training to their employees, [where] they failed to do so" (p. 656). However, there was never a discussion about the merits of this issue, since the case turned on the issue of whether the parents could establish an injury to themselves for the loss of their son (see later discussion under Injury). The case apparently was settled later, and it is still undetermined whether a school would actually be liable in this case.

A case in which the court clearly ruled that the school did not owe an affirmative duty to act to prevent a suicide is *Bogust v. Iverson* (1960). In this case, a troubled college student had several appointments with a professor of education who administered the counseling and testing center. The professor administered personality and aptitude tests to the student and listened to the student's problems. After the professor discontinued the appointments, the student killed herself. The court held that not only was there no duty to prevent the suicide, but there also was no duty to contact the student's parents or refer the student to a counselor. The *Bogust v. Iverson* (1960) ruling stated that

> To hold that a teacher who has had no training, education or experience in medical fields is required to recognize in a student a condition the diagnosis of which is in a specialized and technical medical field, would require a duty beyond reason. (p. 230)

Even given this decision, it would be prudent to have school personnel who work with students trained to assess potentially suicidal students. In the event that a student is suicidal, school policy should state clearly that parents are to be contacted and referrals are to be made.

At this point it is also helpful to note that even for psychiatrists with medical training in suicide, courts rarely, in outpatient settings, find the psychiatrist liable for preventing suicide (Berman & Cohen-Sandler, 1982; Drukteinis, 1985; Howell, 1988; Klein & Glover, 1983; Knuth, 1979; Schwartz, 1971).

A school could be found to have a duty based on a statute that the school has violated. Thus, if your state has a statute requiring that parents or specified officials be contacted when students indicate they are contemplating suicide, failure to comply could lead to a special duty (and automatically a breach of that duty) for purposes of finding negligence. To show a special duty for violation of a statute there are two caveats: (1) the purpose of the statute must have been to protect the person injured and (2) to prevent the kind of injury that occurs. To date no cases have discussed this issue in relation to suicide.

Breach of duty

Even if the plaintiff can establish that a duty existed, it still must be proven that the school breached that duty. "A person or entity will not be held liable for another's suicide unless his conduct falls below the standard of care imposed by law" (Knuth, 1979). That standard is usually governed by what a reasonable person in similar circumstances in a similar community would do. Thus, the school faculty and staff must have acted in a reasonable manner for school personnel in the community or area in a similar situation (Bursztajn, Gutheil, Hamm & Brodsky, 1983).

There are no cases centering on the standard of care that is owed by a school to a potentially suicidal student. However, it is clear from the literature and case law that accurate records indicating how a suicide threat was handled will help prove that the appropriate steps were taken. In addition, school faculty and staff should follow clear policy that directs them to consult with others whenever they are uncertain how to proceed (Bursztajn et al., 1983; Drukteinis, 1985; Knapp & Vandecreek, 1983; Perr, 1985).

Causation

To be liable, the plaintiff would have to establish that the school's breach of duty caused the student's suicide. There are two types of causation: (1) negligent actions that directly caused the injury and (2) negligent actions that indirectly caused the injury. In a suicide situation, the individual's suicide or suicide attempt would be the direct cause and the school's negligence could, at best, be an indirect cause.

In negligence, defendants' actions, although the indirect cause, may be found to have proximately caused the injury when the result was foreseeable. "If the intervening cause [the suicide] is foreseeable, then the chain of causation...is not broken by the independent intervening agency [the suicide], and the original wrongful act will be treated as the proximate cause of the injury" (*Runyon v. Reid*, 1973, p. 948). However, when "the negligence...merely furnished a condition by which the injury was possible and a subsequent independent act [such as suicide] caused the injury" (*Runyon v. Reid*, 1973, p. 948), then the negligence will not be considered the proximate cause.

While this may seem confusing, it is important to remember that when schools follow legally approved policies and procedures with a student who is potentially suicidal (such as contacting parents and referring the student), the faculty and staff's actions will likely not be viewed as having caused the suicide or suicide attempt.

Injury

The plaintiff will be unable to recover for negligence if the type of injury suffered is not compensable. In the case of a suicide attempt, the injury suffered could be compensable (if negligence were proven) to the student, because the student personally suffered the injury. The issue generally arises in this area when parents or siblings attempt to recover for the suicide (and attempted suicide) of the student.

There is some case law supporting the parents' right to recover for a child's suicide. This was the issue actually determined by the court in *Kelson v. City of Springfield* (1985). The court upheld the parents' right to bring suit for loss of their son, stating "the parent-child relationship is constitutionally protected and...governmental interference with it gives rise to...action for damages" (*Kelson v. City of Springfield*, 1985, p. 654). The court found constitutional protection of parental rights, and thus the right to obtain compensation for loss of a child, in both the Fourteenth Amendment (Due Process Clause and Equal Protection Clause) and the Ninth Amendment. Courts consistently have held that "due process must be afforded to a parent prior to state termination of her parental right on grounds of unfitness" (*Kelson v. City of Springfield*, 1985, p. 654).

Since the *Kelson* decision, many courts have upheld parental rights to compensation (*Greene v. City of New York*, 1987; *Smith v. City of Fontana*, 1987). However, the courts have not extended these rights to siblings (*Bell v. City of Milwaukee*, 1984; *de la Cruz LaChapel v. Chevere Ortiz*, 1986). The parental right to recovery was also limited in *Sollars v. City of Albuquerque* (1992), stating, "to state a claim for familial relationships, the defendant must have intended to violate the rights of the family survivor" (p. 362). If the *Sollars* decision is followed, the result would lead to difficulty in parents' proving that they are entitled to compensation for suicide. However, this issue is still unsettled as the U.S. Supreme Court has yet to rule on it.

One final note, according to Drukteinis (1985): as states have become reluctant to "hold the victim criminally responsible, there is...an increasing trend to regard the victim's acts as involuntary and to find someone else responsible either for causing the suicide or failing to prevent it" (p. 77). Thus, to avoid potential liability, policy must be in place that establishes the procedures to be followed by a faculty or staff member aware of a potential suicide.

PRIVACY/CONFIDENTIALITY ISSUES

"Confidentiality is the general legal and ethical obligation of professionals to maintain secrets revealed to them by clients" (Smith, 1986, p. 123). Confidentiality is a priority because it allows the person being counseled in the school setting, the student, to talk freely without fear of the information being disclosed.

Ethical and legal codes require that student information remain confidential. "School counselors have a general ethical and legal responsibility to keep secret any confidential information related to them by students, parents, teachers, and other school officials. Nonetheless, there are some clear exceptions" (Remley, Jr., & Sparkman, 1993, p. 166). When a student is potentially suicidal, an exception to the requirement of confidentiality exists. This exception extends from the duty to warn of potential harm to others, first held in *Tarasoff v. Regents of the University of California* (1976). The duty to notify parents or others about a potentially suicidal patient is a negligence issue and is discussed more extensively in that section. However, it must be stressed that confidentiality not only *should* be breached, but also *must* be breached when a student is potentially suicidal. As Remley, Jr., & Sparkman (1993) state, "when clients present a danger to themselves...set aside...confidentiality and take whatever steps are necessary to prevent students from taking their own lives" (p. 166).

To make certain that confidentiality requirements, and exceptions to those requirements, are met, your school should establish "a clear protocol or policy within the school concerning the transfer of information to parents, school authorities, teachers, the permanent records of the school and to others outside the school" (Smith, 1986, p. 124).

Family Educational and Privacy Rights Act

In the main, student privacy and confidentiality issues are governed by the Family Educational and Privacy Rights Act of 1974 (FERPA). This federal "statute's apparent purpose is to ensure access to educational records for students and parents and to protect the privacy of such records from the public at large" (*Student Press Law Center v. Alexander*, 1991, p. 1228). According to the *Smith v. Duquesne University* (1985) court, "the underlying purpose of FERPA was not to grant individual students a right to privacy or access to educational records, but to stem the growing policy of many institutions to carelessly release student records" (p. 80).

"FERPA provides two fundamental rights to students [and parents]. Students [and parents] are permitted access to their own files, and they may limit access to their files except to a specified list of officials" (Hyman, 1982, p. 569). Although issues involving FERPA arise any time information contained within student records is shared, specific issues may come up when suicide is threatened, attempted, or completed.

The first issue is what student information is protected under FERPA. Any time student records are shared, it is important to consider whether the records are protected under FERPA. The first class of records protected under FERPA is education records. "The term 'education records' means...those records, files, documents, and other materials which—(i) contain information directly related to a student; and (ii) are maintained by an educational agency, or institution or by a person acting for such agency or institution" (FERPA, 1974, 20 USCS 1232g [a] [4] [A], p. 427). This means that any information about a specific student will be considered education records, when it meets the other criteria. According to Baker (1987), education records include "highly subjective, personal and qualitative data such as student grades, health information, counselor's reports, personality profiles, vocational testing results, teacher observations, family-related information and...disciplinary reports (p. 78).

FERPA also lists exceptions to education records. These include "records of instructional, supervisory, and administrative personnel and educational personnel...in the sole possession of the maker...not accessible or revealed to any other person except a substitute" (FERPA, 1974, 20 USCS 1232g [a] [4] [B] [i], p. 427). The second exception is for records kept separately by, and exclusively for, law enforcement agencies of the school. Third, employee records exclusive to the employee are not included. Last, "records created or maintained by a psychologist, physician, or psychiatrist which are used solely for the treatment of the student are exempt" (Hyman, 1982 p. 577-578).

Those records exempted from education records under FERPA are granted "even greater protection" (Baker, 1987), and parents and students will not have access to them. The records exempted because they are the sole possession of the maker remain the personal property of the person making them, as long as the records are not shared and the staff member takes them home. The counselor or school staff member who becomes privy to a suicide threat may wish to include a written record of the threat in the student's file to aid in dissemination of the information without violating FERPA.

FERPA requires parental (or student over 18) consent prior to disclosure of education records. However, there are exceptions to the consent requirement. The two most important exceptions for the school's purposes are: sharing information with "other school officials, including teachers...who...have legitimate educational interests" (FERPA, 1974, 20 USCS 1232g[b][A], p. 428); and "in connection with an emergency, appropriate persons if the knowledge of such information is necessary to protect the health or safety of the student or other persons" (FERPA, 1974, 20 USCS 1232g[b][I], p. 429). Generally, the provision providing for sharing of education records has been interpreted to mean that school staff members may be afforded access on a need-to-know basis; this would enable all members of a suicide crisis team access to the records of a student who is potentially suicidal. The emergency provision provides additional protection for disseminating information to a crisis team. In addition, the emergency provision would allow the school to circulate information to students and staff members to prevent cluster suicides following an attempted or completed suicide.

As discussed previously, when a student is contemplating suicide, the school has a legal obligation to notify the student's parents of the suicidal risk. In the main, FERPA requirements support this obligation. However, if the student is 18 or older, FERPA grants the student "the permission or consent required of and the rights accorded to the parents" (FERPA, 1974, 20 USCS 1232g[d], p. 430). Parents of a potentially suicidal student still should be notified, since the school can rely on the emergency provision that allows sharing education record information to protect student safety.

Although schools can lose federal funding if they violate FERPA, it has been decided consistently that there is no private right of action created by FERPA (*Girardier v. Webster College*, 1977; *Price v. Young*, 1983; *Smith v. Duquesne University*, 1985; *Tarka v. Cunningham*, 1990). This is due, at least in part, to the fact "that FERPA was adopted to address systematic, not individual, violations of students' privacy and confidentiality rights through unauthorized releases of sensitive educational records" (*Smith v. Duquesne University*, 1985, p. 80). However, a cause of action is posible under negligence for violation of FERPA; refer to *Duty* in the Negligence section for further discussion of this issue.

One final piece of advice from Smith (1986): "...some caution should be exercised concerning the maintenance of records. Unnecessary records should not be kept and those that are kept should be secured and couched in language that will not be misunderstood" (p. 123).

Other Causes of Action

Four common law causes of action can be brought against the school "when the statements made concerning the student are untrue or reveal certain things a student may not want revealed" (Eades, 1986, p. 117). The four causes are defamation, public disclosure of private fact, false lights, and intentional infliction of emotional distress.

"The basic elements of a defamation action are...proof of making a statement with a defamatory meaning, either written or oral; and second, proof of some actual or economic damage depending on the type of statement involved" (Eades, 1986, p. 118). However, an absolute defense to defamation is that the statement was true; the person bringing the suit, the plaintiff, must prove that the statement was false. Obviously, schools will want to ensure accuracy of all information released concerning students.

"Public disclosure of private facts, the tort most likely to be committed by an educational institution, has been found applicable only to disclosure through a public medium, such as a newspaper or television" (Hyman, 1982, p. 580). In addition, to maintain a cause of action for public disclosure of private facts requires disclosure of facts that are so private that "the public has no right to know" (Eades, 1986, p. 119) them. Schools must be extremely judicious when providing private information about students to the media.

The cause of action for "false light...requires that the material be published, false, and highly offensive to a reasonable person" (Hyman, 1982, p. 581). Once again, making certain that all information disseminated regarding students is accurate will protect the school.

An action for intentional infliction of emotional distress is available only where the plaintiff "can prove extreme or outrageous conduct on the part of the institution and that the institution intended to cause the severe emotional distress" (Hyman, 1982, p. 581). Thus, only malicious conduct by school staff members would result in a successful suit.

SUICIDE LAWS THROUGHOUT THE UNITED STATES

Most state laws within the United States are derived from English common law. Common law in England considered suicide a serious crime. When death was found to be the result of a suicide, the unfortunate person's body had a stake driven through its heart and was buried under a crossroads (instead of in a graveyard). In addition, the deceased's property was forfeited and given to the government. From the beginning, the United States tended to be less harsh with victims of suicide. A normal burial for the suicide victim has always been allowed. Currently, none of the states or districts requires forfeiture of property, and few ever required forfeiture in the past (Marzen, O'Dowd, Crone, & Balch, 1985).

Currently, the law on suicide varies from state to state. Most states don't consider completed and attempted suicides to be crimes; however, Alabama, Georgia, Idaho, Maryland, Montana, Puerto Rico, Vermont, Virginia, Washington, D.C., and West Virginia are still undecided about whether to continue to regard suicide as a crime. South Carolina alone still considers suicide a felony (Marzen et al., 1985).

Most states find an individual who administers poison, deceives, persuades, or coerces another into suicide guilty of murder. However, when the issue is aiding, assisting, soliciting and encouraging, states vary on the severity of the crime (Marzen et al., 1985).

In Alaska, Arkansas, Colorado, Kentucky, Missouri, New York, Oregon, Pennsylvania, and Wisconsin, statutes allow an observer to use force to prevent a suicide. In addition, courts throughout the United States consistently have upheld murder convictions when a person attempting suicide kills an observer who is trying to prevent the act (Marzen et al., 1985).

Of particular concern to schools may be the laws governing involuntary commitment of potentially suicidal students. Only Arkansas and New Jersey provide for commitment for a person who is suicidal, or has attempted suicide, without a requirement that the person have a mental illness or disability. South Dakota requires a finding of behavior that shows that the person is a danger to self or others. The remainder of the states require a finding of mental illness, mental disability, mental impairment, or mental disorder coupled with a likelihood that the person is a danger to self or others, or likely to cause serious harm/injury to self or others (Marzen et al., 1985).

As this review illustrates, laws regarding suicide vary greatly from state to state. In addition, state courts vary in their interpretations of similar language. Thus, the best advice is still to seek legal counsel whenever suicide issues arise.

GENERAL LEGAL ISSUES

- **SCHOOL POLICY**

- **DOCUMENTATION**

- **NEGLIGENCE**

- **PRIVACY/CONFIDENTIALITY ISSUES**

SCHOOL POLICY ISSUES

- Policies must be in writing!

- Policies must cover all issues surrounding student suicide, including confidentiality, suicide attempts, and postvention.

- Policies must be disseminated school-wide or district-wide.

- All faculty and staff must be aware of the policies and be required to follow them.

- Policies must be written, or approved, by school attorney.

DOCUMENTATION

THOROUGH DOCUMENTATION OF ALL INFORMATION SURROUNDING STUDENTS' POTENTIAL FOR SUICIDE:

- Written discussion of factors indicating suicide potential.

- Documentation of the steps taken by the faculty or staff member (as required by school/district policy) in response to potential suicide.

- Documentation of parent contact made pursuant to the suicide potential.

- Completion of any suicide assessment form required by school or district.

- Documentation of any follow-up with student.

NEGLIGENCE

- The school must provide supervisory care of students at the same level as a concerned parent.

- Failure to prevent suicide, based on lack of action when faculty or staff member was aware of student's potential for suicide.

- Failure to follow school policy when student indicates suicidal preoccupation.

- Failure to document procedures followed with a suicidal student.

- Failure to notify parent when faculty or staff member has reason to believe a student is at risk of suicide.

- Violation of a statute that protects students at risk of suicide.

PRIVACY AND CONFIDENTIALITY

- Confidentiality requires maintaining secrets revealed by students, as long as the student is not at risk of harming self or others.

FAMILY EDUCATIONAL AND PRIVACY RIGHTS ACT:

- Governs most documents related to each student.

- Two fundamental rights of parents/students:

    (1) access to child's/own records

    (2) limited access by others

- Student records are any records, files, documents maintained by the school/district containing information directly related to student.

PRIVACY AND CONFIDENTIALITY

FAMILY EDUCATIONAL AND PRIVACY RIGHTS ACT:

- Emergency provision enables sharing of student records to protect the health and safety of the student or others.

- Student records may be shared by faculty/staff members on a need-to-know basis.

- Records kept in the sole possession of faculty or staff members are inaccessible to parents/ students.

REFERENCES

Achenbach, T. M. (1983). *Manual for child behavior checklist and revised child behavior profile.* Burlington: University of Vermont, Department of Psychiatry.

Achenbach, T. M., & Edelbrock, C. (1986). *Manual for the teacher's report form and teacher version of the child behavior profile.* Burlington: University of Vermont, Department of Psychiatry.

Achenbach, T. M., & Edelbrock, C. (1987). *Manual for youth self-report and profile.* Burlington: University of Vermont, Department of Psychiatry.

American Association of Suicidology. (1987). *Postvention guidelines.* Denver: Author.

American Psychiatric Association. (1987). *Diagnostic and statistical manual of mental disorders* (rev. 3rd ed.). Washington, DC: Author.

Baker, M. G. (1987). The teacher's need to know versus the student's right to privacy. *Journal of Law & Education, 16*(1), 71–91.

Ballard v. Polly, 387 F. Supp. 895 (1975).

Beck, A. T., Ward, C., Mendelson, M., Mock, J., & Erbaugh, J. (1961). An inventory for measuring depression. *Archives of General Psychiatry, 4,* 561–571.

Bell v. City of Milwaukee, 746 F.2d 1205 (7th Cir. 1984).

Berkovitz, I. H. (1987). Building a suicide prevention climate in schools. *Adolescent Psychiatry, 14,* 500–510.

Berman, A. L., & Cohen-Sandler, R. (1982). Suicide and the standard of care: Optimal v. acceptable. *Suicide and Life-Threatening Behavior, 12*(2), 114–122.

Berman, A. L., & Jobes, D. A. (1991). *Adolescent suicide. Assessment and intervention.* Washington, DC: American Psychological Association.

Bigrar, J., Gauthier, Y., Bouchard, C., & Jasse, Y. (1966). On the depressive illness in childhood: Suicidal attempts in adolescent girls. A preliminary study. *Canadian Psychiatric Association Journal, 11*(Suppl.), 275–282.

Bogust v. Iverson, 102 N.W.2d 228 (1960).

Bursztajn, H., Gutheil, T. G., Hamm, R. M., & Brodsky, A. (1983). Subjective data and suicide assessment in the light of recent legal developments. Part II: Clinical uses of legal standards in the interpretation of subjective data. *International Journal of Law and Psychiatry, 6,* 331–350.

Cantor, P. (1976). Personality characteristics found among youthful female suicide attempters. *Journal of Abnormal Psychology, 85,* 324–329.

Capuzzi, D. (1986). Adolescent suicide: Prevention and intervention. *Counseling and Human Development, 19*(2), 1–9.

Capuzzi, D. (1988). *Counseling and intervention strategies for adolescent suicide prevention* (Contract No. 400-86-0014). Ann Arbor, MI: ERIC Counseling and Personnel Services Clearinghouse.

Capuzzi, D., & Golden, L. (Eds.). (1988). *Preventing adolescent suicide.* Muncie, IN: Accelerated Development, Inc.

Cull, J., & Gill, W. (1982). *Suicide probability scale manual.* Los Angeles: Western Psychological Services.

Curran, D. F. (1987). *Adolescent suicidal behavior.* Washington, DC: Hemisphere Publishing.

de la Cruz LaChapel v. Chevere Ortiz, 637 F. Supp. 43 (D. Puerto Rico 1986).

Davis, P. A. (1983). *Suicidal adolescents.* Springfield, IL: Charles C. Thomas.

Drukteinis, A. M. (1985). Psychiatric perspectives on civil liability for suicide. *Bulletin of American Academy of Psychiatry Law, 13*(1), 71–83.

Eades, R. W. (1986). The school counselor or psychologist and problems of defamation. *Journal of Law & Education, 15*(1), 117–120.

Eddy, D. M., Wolpert, R. L., & Rosenberg, M. L. (1987). Estimating the effectiveness of interventions to prevent youth suicides. *Medical Care, 25*(12), Supplement, S57–S65.

Ellis, A. (1979). The practice of rational-emotive therapy. In A. Ellis & J. Whiteley (Eds.), *Theoretical and empirical foundations of rational-emotive therapy* (pp. 61–100). Monterey, CA: Brooks/Cole Publishing Company.

Faigel, H. (1966). Suicide among young persons: A review of its incidence and causes, and methods for its prevention. *Clinical Pediatrics, 5*, 187–190.

Family Educational and Privacy Rights Act of 1974, 20 U.S.C. 1232g (1974).

Garland, A. F., & Zigler, E. (1993). Adolescent suicide prevention: Current research and social policy implications. *American Psychologist, 48*(2), 169-182.

Girardier v. Webster College, 563 F.2d 1267 (8th Cir. 1977).

Greene v. City of New York, 675 F. Supp. 110 (S.D. N.Y. 1987).

Gysbers, N. C., & Henderson, P. (1994). *Developing and managing your school guidance program.* Alexandria, VA: ACA.

Hafen, B. Q. (Ed.). (1972). *Self-destructive behavior.* Minneapolis, MN: Burgess.

Hafen, B. Q., & Frandsen, K. J. (1986). *Youth suicide: Depression and loneliness.* Provo, UT: Behavioral Health Associates.

Hamilton, M. (1967). Development of a rating scale for primary depressive illness. *British Journal of Social and Clinical Psychology, 6*, 278–296.

Hayes, M. L., & Sloat, R. S. (1988). Preventing suicide in learning disabled children and adolescents. *Academic Therapy, 24*(2), 221–230.

Herjanic, B., & Reich, W. (1982). Development of a structured psychiatric interview for children: Agreement between child and parent on individual symptoms. *Journal of Abnormal Child Psychology, 10*, 307–324.

Hetzel, S., Winn, V., & Tolstoshev, H. (1991). Loss & change: New directions in death education for adolescents. *Journal of Adolescence, 14*, 323–334.

Howell, J. A. (1988). Civil liability for suicide: An analysis of the causation issue. *Arizona State Law Journal*, 573–615.

Hussain, S. A., & Vandiver, K. T. (1984). *Suicide in children and adolescents.* New York: SP Medical and Scientific Books.

Hyman, U. H. (1982). The Family Educational Rights and Privacy Act of 1974 and the college record systems of the future. *Computer Law Journal, III*, 553–618.

Jacobs, J. (1971). *Adolescent suicide.* New York: Wiley-Interscience.

Jacobziner, H. (1965). Attempted suicides in adolescents by poisoning. *Journal of the American Medical Association, 191* (1), 101–105.

Josef, N.C., Kinkel, R. J., & Bailey, C. W. (1985). Suicidal ideation in school-age adolescents. U.S. Congress. House. Subcommittee on Elementary, Secondary, and Vocational Education. Hearings on H.R. 1099. 55–65.

Johnson, S. W., & Maile, L. J. (1987). *Suicide and the schools: A handbook for prevention, intervention, and rehabilitation.* Springfield, IL: Charles C. Thomas.

Kelson v. City of Springfield, 767 F.2d 651 (1985).

Kidsrights catalog. (1993). Mount Dora, FL: Kidsrights.

Kiev, A. (1977). *The suicidal patient.* Chicago: Nelson-Hall.

Klein, J. L., & Glover, S. I. (1983). Psychiatric malpractice. *International Journal of Law and Psychiatry, 6*, 131–137.

Knapp, S. & Vandecreek, L. (1983). Malpractice risks with suicidal patients. *Psychotherapy: Theory, Research and Practice, 20*(3), 274–280.

Knuth, M. O. (1979). Civil liability for causing or failing to prevent suicide. *Loyola of Los Angeles Law Review, 12*, 965–991.

Kovacs, M., Beck, A., & Weissman, A. (1975). The use of suicidal motives in the psychotherapy of attempted suicides. *American Journal of Psychotherapy, 29*, 363–368.

Krumboltz, J. D., & Thoresen, C. E. (Eds.). (1976). *Counseling methods.* New York: Holt, Rinehart & Winston.

Lang, M., & Tisher, M. (1978). *Children's Depression Scale.* Victoria, Australia: Australian Council for Educational Research.

Lawrence, M. T., & Ureda, J. R. (1990). Student recognition of and response to suicidal peers. *Suicide and Life-Threatening Behavior, 20*(2), 164–176.

Lazarus, A. (1976). *Multi-modal behavior therapy.* New York: Springer.

Lefkowitz, M. M., & Tesiny, E. P. (1980). Assessment of childhood depression. *Journal of Consulting and Clinical Psychology, 48*, 43–50.

Males, M. (1991). Teen suicide and changing cause-of-death certification, 1953–1987. *Suicide and Life-Threatening Behavior, 21*(3), 245-259.

Marzen, T. J., O'Dowd, M. K., Crone, D., & Balch, T. J. (1985). Suicide a constitutional right? *Duquesne Law Review, 24*(1), 1–242.

McAnarney, E. R. (1979). Adolescent and young adult suicide in the United States—A reflection of societal unrest? *Adolescence, 14* (56), 765–774.

McBride v. State. 294 N.Y.S.2d 265 (1968).

McCoy, K. (1982). *Coping with teenage depression: A parent's guide.* New York: NAL.

McWhirter, J. J., & Kigin, T. J. (1988). Depression. In D. Capuzzi & L. Golden (Eds.), *Preventing adolescent suicide* (pp. 149–186). Muncie, IN: Accelerated Development, Inc.

Mehan, P J., Lamb, J. A., Saltzman, L. E., & O'Carroll, P. W. (1992). Attempted suicide among young adults: Progress toward a meaningful estimate of prevalence. *American Journal of Psychiatry, 149*(1), 41–44.

Meneese, W. B., & Yutrzenka, B. A. (1990). Correlates of suicidal ideation among rural adolescents. *Suicide and Life-Threatening Behavior, 20*(3), 206–212.

Mulder, M. M., Methorst, G. J., & Diekstra, R. F. (1989). Prevention of suicidal behavior in adolescents: The role and training of teachers. *Crisis, 10*(1), 36–51.

Nelson, F. L., Farberow, N. L., & Litman, R. E. (1988). Youth suicide in California: A comparative study of perceived causes and interventions. *Community Mental Health Journal, 24*(1), 31–42.

Otto, V. (1972). Suicidal acts by children and adolescents: A follow-up study. *Acta Psychiatrica Scandinavica, 233* (Supplement), 5–123.

Peach, L., & Reddick, T. L. (1991). Counselors can make a difference in preventing adolescent suicide. *The School Counselor, 39*, 107–110.

Peck, D. (1983). The last moments of life: Learning to cope. *Deviant Behavior, 4*, 313–342.

Perr, I. N. (1985). Suicide litigation and risk management: A review of 32 cases. *The Bulletin of the American Academy of Psychiatry and the Law, 13*, 209–219.

Petti, T. A. (1983). The assessment of depression in young children. *Journal of Children in Contemporary Society, 15*, 19–28.

Poznanski, E. O., Cook, S. C., & Carroll, B. J. (1979). LA depression rating scale for children. *Pediatrics, 64*, 442–450.

Price v. Young, 580 F. Supp. 1 (1983).

Remley, Jr., T. P., & Sparkman, L. B. (1993). Student suicides: The counselor's limited legal liability. *The School Counselor, 40*, 164–169.

Reynolds, William M. (1992). *Internalizing disorders in children and adolescents*. New York: John Wiley & Sons, Inc.

Rodesh, C. J. (undated). *Youth suicide attempts and the emergency room*. Unpublished paper. Green Bay, WI: St. Vincent Hospital.

Rosenberg, M. L., Davidson, L. E., Smith, J. C., Berman, A. L., Buzbee, H., Gantner, G., Gay, G. A., Moore-Lewis, B., Mills, D. H., Murray, D., O'Carroll, P. W., & Jobes, D. (1988). Operational criteria for the determination of suicide. *Journal of Forensic Sciences, 33*(6), 1445–1446.

Ross, C. (1980). Mobilizing schools for suicide prevention. *Suicide and Life-Threatening Behavior, 10*, 239–243.

Runyon v. Reid, Okl., 510 P.2d 943 (1973).

Sandoval, J., Davis, J. M., & Wilson, M. P. (1987). An overview of the school-based prevention of adolescent suicide. *Special Services in the Schools, 3*(3–4), 103–120.

Schneidman, E., Farbverow, N., & Litman, R. (1976). *The psychology of suicide*. New York: Jason Aronson.

Schwartz, V. E. (1971). Civil liability for causing suicide: A synthesis of law a psychiatry. *Vanderbilt Law Review, 24*(2), 217–256.

Shaffer, D., Garland, A., Gould, M., Fisher, P., & Trautman, P. (1988). Preventing teenage suicide: A critical review. *Journal of the American Academy of Child and Adolescent Psychiatry, 27*(6), 675–687.

Silbert, K. L., & Berry, G. L. (1991). Psychological effects of a suicide prevention unit on adolescents' levels of stress, anxiety and hopelessness: Implications for counselling psychologists. *Counselling Psychology Quarterly, 4*(1), 45–58.

Smith, S. R. (1986). Privacy, dangerousness and counselors. *Journal of Law & Education, 15*(1), 121–130.

Smith v. City of Fontana, 818 F.2d 1411 (9th Cir. 1987).

Smith v. Duquesne University, 612 F. Supp. 72 (D.C. Pa. 1985).

Sollars v. City of Albuquerque, 794 F. Supp. 360 (D. N.M. 1992).

Sommes, B. (1984). The troubled teen: Suicide, drug use, and running away. *Women and Health, 9*, 117–141.

Stefanowski-Harding, S. (1990). Suicide and the school counselor. Child suicide: A review of the literature and implications for school counselors. *The School Counselor, 37*, 328–336.

Stein, M., & Davis, J. (1982). *Therapies for adolescents*. San Francisco: Jossey-Bass.

Stillion, J., McDowell, E., & Shamblin, J. (1984). The suicide attitude vignette experience: A method for measuring adolescent attitudes toward suicide. *Death Education, 8*, 65–81.

Student Press Law Center v. Alexander, 778 F. Supp. 1227 (D. D.C. 1991).

Sudak, H., Ford, A., & Rushforth, N. (1984). Adolescent suicide: An overview. *American Journal of Psychotherapy, 38*(3), 350–369.

Tarasoff v. Regents of the University of California, 42 Cal. 3d 425, P.2d 334, 131 Cal. Rptr. 14 (1976).

Tarka v. Cunningham, 917 F.2d 890 (5th Cir. 1990).

Truckman, J., & Connon, H. E. (1962). Attempted suicides in adolescents. *American Journal of Psychiatry, 119*(3), 228–232.

Velkoff, P., & Huberty, T. J. (1988). Thinking patterns and motivation. In D. Capuzzi & L. Golden (Eds.), *Preventing adolescent suicide* (pp. 111–147). Muncie, IN: Accelerated Development, Inc.

Vital Statistics of the United States 1981: Volume II—Mortality, Part A (1983). U. S. Department of Health and Human Services, Public Health Service, Centers for Disease Control, National Center for Health Statistics.

Vital Statistics of the United States 1981: Volume II—Mortality, Part B (1983). U. S. Department of Health and Human Services, Public Health Service, Centers for Disease Control, National Center for Health Statistics.

Vital Statistics of the United States 1982: Volume II—Mortality, Part B (1984). U. S. Department of Health and Human Services, Public Health Service, Centers for Disease Control, National Center for Health Statistics.

Vital Statistics of the United States 1983: Volume II—Mortality, Part A (1985). U. S. Department of Health and Human Services, Public Health Service, Centers for Disease Control, National Center for Health Statistics.

Vital Statistics of the United States 1983: Volume II—Mortality, Part B (1985). U. S. Department of Health and Human Services, Public Health Service, Centers for Disease Control, National Center for Health Statistics.

Vital Statistics of the United States 1984: Volume II—Mortality, Part A (1986). U. S. Department of Health and Human Services, Public Health Service, Centers for Disease Control, National Center for Health Statistics.

Vital Statistics of the United States 1984: Volume II—Mortality, Part B (1986). U. S. Department of Health and Human Services, Public Health Service, Centers for Disease Control, National Center for Health Statistics.

Vital Statistics of the United States 1985: Volume II—Mortality, Part A (1987). U. S. Department of Health and Human Services, Public Health Service, Centers for Disease Control, National Center for Health Statistics.

Vital Statistics of the United States 1985: Volume II Mortality, Part B (1987). U. S. Department of Health and Human Services, Public Health Service, Centers for Disease Control, National Center for Health Statistics.

Vital Statistics of the United States 1986: Volume II—Mortality, Part A (1988). U. S. Department of Health and Human Services, Public Health Service, Centers for Disease Control, National Center for Health Statistics.

Vital Statistics of the United States 1986: Volume II—Mortality, Part B (1988). U. S. Department of Health and Human Services, Public Health Service, Centers for Disease Control, National Center for Health Statistics.

Vital Statistics of the United States 1987: Volume II—Mortality, Part A (1989). U. S. Department of Health and Human Services, Public Health Service, Centers for Disease Control, National Center for Health Statistics.

Vital Statistics of the United States 1987: Volume II—Mortality, Part B (1989). U. S. Department of Health and Human Services, Public Health Service, Centers for Disease Control, National Center for Health Statistics.

Vital Statistics of the United States 1988: Volume II—Mortality, Part A (1990). U. S. Department of Health and Human Services, Public Health Service, Centers for Disease Control, National Center for Health Statistics.

Vital Statistics of the United States 1988: Volume II—Mortality, Part B (1990). U. S. Department of Health and Human Services, Public Health Service, Centers for Disease Control, National Center for Health Statistics.

Vital Statistics of the United States 1989: Volume II—Mortality, Part A (1991). U. S. Department of Health and Human Services, Public Health Service, Centers for Disease Control, National Center for Health Statistics.

Wirt, R. D., Lachar, D., Klinedinst, J., & Seat, P. D. (1977). *Multidimensional description of child personality: A manual for the personality inventory for children.* Los Angeles: Western Psychological Services.

NOTES

NOTES